KU-460-615

Global Skill Shortages

To our spouses Judy and Ingrid

Global Skill Shortages

Malcolm S. Cohen
Employment Research Corporation
Ann Arbor, MI, USA

and

Mahmood A. Zaidi
University of Minnesota
Minneapolis, MN, USA

Edward Elgar
Cheltenham, UK • Northampton, MA, USA

Published by
Edward Elgar Publishing Limited
Glensanda House
Montpellier Parade
Cheltenham
Glos GL50 1UA
UK

Edward Elgar Publishing, Inc.
136 West Street
Suite 202
Northampton
Massachusetts 01060
USA

A catalogue record for this book
is available from the British Library

Library of Congress Cataloguing in Publication Data
Cohen, Malcolm S.
Global skill shortages / Malcolm S. Cohen and Mahmood A. Zaidi.
p. cm.
Includes index.
1. Labor supply. 2. Skilled labor–Supply and demand. 3. Globalization.
I. Zaidi, Mahmood A. II. Title.

HD5706 .C59 2002
331.11'422–dc21

2002019655

ISBN 1 84064 520 2

Printed and bound in Great Britain by Biddles Ltd, *www.biddles.co.uk*

Contents

List of figures vi

List of tables vii

1 Introduction 1

2 Theoretical aspects of skill shortages 4

3 Globalization and skill shortages 16

4 Skill shortage studies in selected countries 25

5 Shortage indicators by occupation and country 36

6 Factors correlated with shortages 59

7 Coping with skill shortages 92

8 Concluding remarks 96

Appendix: Detailed country indicators 98

Index 136

List of figures

2.1	Static view of shortages	5
2.2	Dynamic view of shortages	6
5.1	Relationship between indicators – France	56
6.1	Legislators, senior officials and managers	68
6.2	Professionals	70
6.3	Technicians and associate professionals residuals	72
6.4	Clerks residuals	73
6.5	Service workers and shop and market sales workers residuals	75
6.6	Skilled agricultural and fishery workers residuals	76
6.7	Craft and related trades workers residuals	78
6.8	Plant and machine operators and assemblers residuals	79
6.9	Elementary occupations	80
6.10	Production and operations department managers	83
6.11	College, university and higher education teaching professionals	86

List of tables

3.1	Total United States trade 1991–99 (millions of dollars)	17
3.2	United States trade with selected countries, 1999 (millions of dollars)	18
3.3	Annual growth rate of foreign direct investment (FDI) 1986–98	19
3.4	Direct investment position for 1999 (millions of dollars)	19
3.5	What makes a company 'American?'	22
4.1	Job openings by occupation group in the Twin Cities of Minnesota, April–June 2000	32
5.1	Summary of occupation groups	40–1
5.2	Employment growth indicator	42
5.3	Unemployment rate indicator	43
5.4	Wage growth indicator	44
5.5	Training indicator	45
5.6	Indicator averages for major occupational groups	47–8
5.7	Occupations with high indicator scores	50
5.8	Occupations with low indicator scores	51
5.9	Indicator scores of detailed skilled occupations mentioned as shortage occupations in Chapter 4	52

5.10 Correlation coefficients and Cronbach's Alpha – summary occupations 54

5.11 Correlation coefficients and Cronbach's Alpha – detailed occupations 55

5.12 Summary occupations – with observations on employment growth and wage growth 56

6.1 EIU indicators, their definitions and predicted signs 61–2

6.2 Regression coefficients – summary occupations 66–7

6.3 Regression coefficients – legislators, senior officials and managers 82

6.4 Regression coefficients – professionals 84

6.5 Regression coefficients – technicians and associate professionals 87

6.6 Regression coefficients – service workers and shop and market sales workers 89

6.7 Regression coefficients – craft and related trades workers 90

6.8 Regression coefficients – plant and machine operators and assemblers 91

1. Introduction

The global economy has experienced one of the most tumultuous periods in recent history during the writing of this book. Global skill shortages which were present in 1998 became more acute as we entered the new millennium. By 2001 the global economy entered a slowdown. The attacks upon New York City and Washington, DC on 11 September 2001 further exacerbated the effects of an already weakened economy, contributing to a rapid increase in lay-offs, an increase in global unemployment rates, a drop in corporate profits, a decline in gross domestic product growth and a further decline in global equity prices. As we go to press, it seems that a good monetary and fiscal policy over the past year has been putting the US economy back on track (Feldstein, 2002).

Throughout history, global economies have risen and fallen. We are confident that as the global economy recovers, skill shortages will once again reappear. Although our research largely covers the period 1995–98, previous research conducted in the United States found skill shortages in some occupations even during the economic downturn in 1991.

We believe the cause of skill shortages, their measurement during 1995–98 and variation across countries will again become relevant as we head into new periods of skill shortages in the twenty-first century.

In recent decades, many macroeconomic changes have occurred in market economies that have had significant microeconomic implications (Siebert and Zaidi, 1996; Erickson, Kimbell and Mitchell, 1997). Variables such as the unemployment rate play a major role in macroeconomic theory (Zaidi, 1991). As the unemployment rate falls the economy approaches full employment. However our research suggests that even at high unemployment rates, skill shortages exist. Skill shortages in certain occupations have been recognized as a problem in times of expansion as well as contraction.

Generally concerns about skill shortages increase when rapid economic growth has been sustained for a number of years. In the initial period of recovery following a downturn, labour demand can be met by slack labour. After the slack labour becomes employed, shortages can emerge as a problem. The economic cycle does not, however, have the same effect on all occupations. Many variables determine whether shortages will actually occur in a given occupation. Shortages do not have to be country-wide in scope. They can exist in a region of a country, in an industry or even in a sub-specialty of an occupation. These shortages can be bottlenecks to economic growth.

Unfortunately there is no generally agreed upon method for measuring skill shortages. This book explores various aspects of skill shortages, develops a methodology of measuring skill shortages by occupation and applies it to measure shortages using data collected from 19 countries.

Countries from North America, Latin America, Europe and the Pacific region were studied to obtain geographic diversity. The specific countries included were the United States, Canada, Chile, Mexico, Austria, Belgium, Denmark, France, Germany, Greece, Italy, Portugal, Spain, Sweden, the United Kingdom, Australia, Japan, Singapore and the Republic of Korea.

The study was limited to developed and emerging economies where data were more readily available. In order to include a country in our study a consistent time series of either employment or wage data was required. Some countries changed occupational classification systems in the middle of the period of our study and therefore could not be included. In addition, occupational estimates could not be obtained if the country's population was below a certain size. For example, Israel changed its occupational classification in 1997 and has a smaller population and was thereby excluded.

In Chapter 2, a theoretical framework is developed which considers the special factors that make labour markets different from other types of markets. It counters the objection that skill shortages cannot exist any time since increased wages will automatically bring supply and demand into equilibrium. Chapter 3 briefly discusses the forces which drive globalization and make economies interdependent. Chapter 4 summarizes skill shortage studies for the period 1995–98 for the specific countries and regions discussed in this book. Chapter 5 explains and measures the skill shortage indicators for the 19 countries. This is followed by a comparative analysis of the specific and overall factors correlated with skill shortages in Chapter 6. In Chapter 7, we consider how companies have been coping with skill shortages in the short term. Chapter 8 contains our concluding remarks.

It is a pleasure for us to acknowledge the assistance and advice of many people who so patiently and generously assisted us during the preparation of this book. We are especially grateful to Teresa Fulimeni Collier for providing excellent research throughout the writing of the book. We wish to thank Calvin D. Siebert and Brian McCall for reviewing all or part of the manuscript and providing excellent comments. We want to thank Laura Steiner and Sarahjoy Crewe for editorial comments. We appreciate the many individuals in participating countries who provided us with data.

Jean-Pierre Garson and Norman Bowers of the OECD provided many useful suggestions. Staff from both Eurostat and ILO provided us with data on multiple countries. The authors wish to thank George Nezis, Abigail Sanford, Jacqueline Mercer, Hua Wang and Lena Ulvi for research assistance and Adrienne Schiff for editorial assistance in preparing the book. We wish to thank our families, Ingrid, Judy, Ilona, Laura and Randy. The authors wish to thank Susan Hammant, desk editor, Julie Leppard, head of editorial and production services and Alan Strurmer, acquisition editor, all from Edward Elgar Publishing, for their assistance throughout the publication process.

REFERENCES

Erickson, Christopher L., L. Kimbell and D.J.B. Mitchell (1997), 'The Macro Side of Human Resource Management', in D. Lewin, D.J.B. Mitchell and M.A. Zaidi (eds), *The Human Resource Management Handbook*, **3**, 259–86, Greenwich, CT: JAI Press.

Feldstein, Martin (2002), 'Tax Cuts, Rate Cuts Put the Economy Back on Track', *Wall Street Journal*, 239 (50), A18.

Siebert, Calvin D. and M. Zaidi (1996), 'Employment, Trade and Foreign Investment Effects of NAFTA', *Minnesota Journal of Global Trade*, **5** (2), 333–55.

Zaidi, Mahmood A. (1991), 'Some Reflections on Theories of Unemployment in the North American Context', *The North American Review of Economics and Finance*, **2** (1), 1–22.

2. Theoretical aspects of skill shortages

This chapter reviews some of the theoretical literature on skill shortages.[1] It is important to point out at the outset that there is some discussion in the literature about the precise definition of skill shortages by occupation (Bosworth and Warren, 1992; Muysken, 1994). One of the main arguments here is that the term 'shortage' is imprecise. In a discussion of skill shortages one needs to consider skills as encompassing economic and institutional factors as well as innate abilities and personal characteristics. Booth and Snower (1996) blame the problem on insufficient incentives for people to acquire skills. Solow (1990) argues that the market clearing mechanism applied to labour markets has failed to explain the presence of unemployment. In other words, labour cannot be viewed as a commodity and labour markets do not behave in the same way as product markets. Furthermore, the traditional general equilibrium theory cannot easily justify the existence of skill shortages.[2]

This is not the place for an extensive discussion of general equilibrium theory as applied to labour markets.[3] Our review is limited to a presentation of important concepts associated with static and dynamic skill shortages and explanations for the failure of labour markets to clear. The efficiency wage theory, the insider–outsider approach, barriers to mobility and the notion of path dependence are four concepts that provide explanations for the failure of labour markets to clear.

STATIC SHORTAGES

The existence of a skill shortage in a traditional and partial equilibrium framework can be easily determined. If the demand for labour in an occupation exceeds supply then a shortage exists. According to a simple static model of the labour market, competitive market forces will drive up the wage rate eliminating the shortage. This model is illustrated in Figure 2.1 showing the supply and demand curves for labour services for a given occupation in a particular labour market. For example, W^0 is the wage level for a certain occupation associated with the amount of labour demand L^0_D and the amount of labour supply L^0_S. The excess labour demand, $L^0_D - L^0_S$, is a measure of skill shortage. Bosworth and Warren (1992) suggested that the magnitude of labour shortages could also be measured in percentage terms. The shortage in this case could be defined as $(L^0_D - L^0_S)/L^A$, where L^A is $(L^0_D + L^0_S)/2$. Irrespective of the excess demand measures used in the analysis, any time a market is not in equilibrium, the excess demand for labour will drive the wage rate up to W^*, the market clearing wage at which employer and employee will exchange labour services. At this wage, labour supply and labour demand will equal L^*.

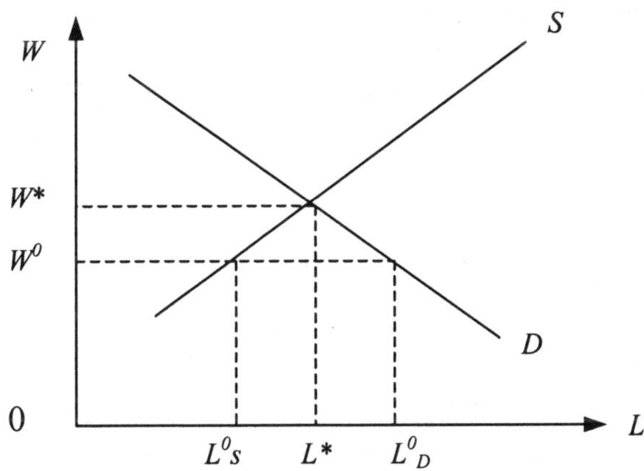

Figure 2.1 Static view of shortages

DYNAMIC SHORTAGES

The static view of labour markets illustrated in Figure 2.1 does not take adequate account of the dynamics involved in labour market adjustment. Employers react to changing labour market conditions in a variety of ways such as increasing wages or increasing search costs. Employers do not have perfect information about market conditions and job seekers do not have perfect information about available jobs. There is a continuous process of adjustment to changing conditions with many factors interacting at once. Labour market dynamics can explain skill shortages if adjustment speed is slow or if there are barriers to adjustment.

A dynamic view of labour market adjustment was introduced by Arrow and Capron (1959). According to these authors, 'a steady upward shift in the demand curve will produce a shortage, that is, a situation in which there are unfilled vacancies in positions where salaries are the same as those currently being paid in others of the same type and quality'. This concept is illustrated in Figure 2.2. Thus shortages can be caused by continuous shifts in the demand curve in the process of adjustment to changing conditions. Similarly, unfilled vacancies in specific positions cause shortages when 'the number of workers available increases less rapidly than the number demanded at the salaries paid in the recent past' (Blank and Stigler, 1957). Alternatively, shortages exist when the existence of individual sources of disequilibria leads to slow adjustment speed and imposes barriers to adjustment (Trutko et al., 1991). The dynamic view suggests that the labour market mechanism could explain labour shortages if and only if the significant role of restrictions, the interaction of other relevant facts and the idiosyncrasies of the labour market are recognized and considered.

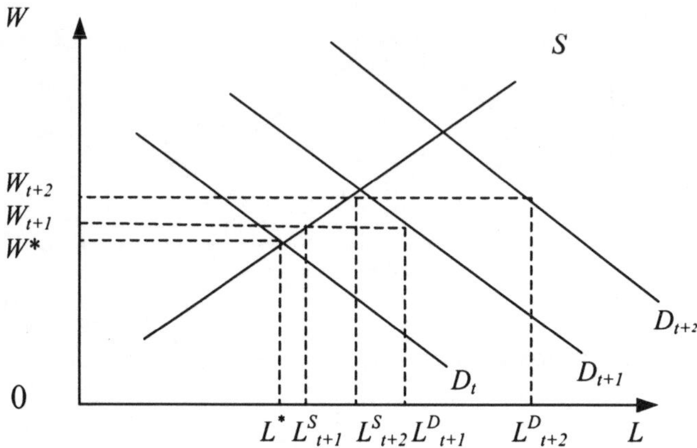

Figure 2.2 Dynamic view of shortages

Figure 2.2 shows this dynamic view of skill shortages. Instead of the wage adjusting toward a long-run equilibrium position, the equilibrium itself will move because of the continuous shifts of the labour demand curve, when the concept of time period (*t*) is added into the labour market framework. Starting from market clearing status W^* and L^*, with the steady increase of labour demand the demand curve shifts outward, $L^* \rightarrow L^D_{t+1} \rightarrow L^D_{t+2}$. Although the wage makes corresponding upward adjustments to meet the extra need of labour demand the rate change is slower than the rapidly changing market $(W^* \rightarrow W_{t+1} \rightarrow W_{t+2})$, therefore the labour shortage exists and increases over time.

EFFICIENCY WAGE THEORY

According to efficiency wage theories output is not only a positive function of labour inputs but it is also assumed to depend on the variance of wages paid in the firm (Akerlof, and Yellen, 1986). They assume:

$$q=e(s^2[w])f(L_1,L_2); e' < 0, f>0 \tag{2.1}$$

where q is output, L_1 and L_2 are employment in occupations 1 and 2, e is a function of the variance in wages paid, w is wages, f is a function of labour inputs and s^2 is the variance. According to this model a worker's productivity is adversely affected by increases in the relative wage of workers in other occupations in the firm.

Therefore if a labour shortage develops in one occupation there may be a limit to which the firm can increase the wages of workers in that occupation. A selective increase in wages is inefficient for the firm because it increases the wage gap across occupations and reduces the productivity of workers in other occupations.

INSIDER–OUTSIDER THEORY

According to the insider–outsider theory (Lindbeck and Snower, 1988, 2001; Solow, 1990) firms may not want to pay outsiders more than they pay insiders in order to attract workers in short supply, for two reasons. Firstly, they would have to adjust the wages of insiders and it may not be economical to increase the wages of all workers in the firm. Secondly, a replacement of insiders with outsiders would deplete the firm of its specific talent. Therefore the insiders within the firm are treated differently to the outsiders not yet in the firm. There may be a limit to which the wages of workers in some occupations fluctuate in order to eliminate shortages. Furthermore, a social norm may exist which prevents unemployed workers from offering their services at less than the market price. Job seekers accepting lower wages will be employed, but they also understand that the result of their behaviour could be a lower wage for all workers in that job category. They may resist lowering their reservation wage offer when they are unemployed because they will be better off with some unemployment at present, but a higher wage when they are employed.

LABOUR MOBILITY

The existence of economic or non-economic barriers to mobility of the labour force may affect the adjustment process in the labour market (Gallaway, 1963; Zaidi, 1969; Padoa-Schioppa, 1991). In a growing economy, particular industries, enterprises or occupations may expand or contract because they are more or less efficient than their competitors. Expanding sectors of the economy, needing more workers, tend to raise wages and contracting sectors tend to do the opposite. According to conventional economic theory, if there is sufficient mobility and movement costs are not high, workers would move from contracting to expanding sectors. The excess supply of labour is quickly absorbed by those parts of the economy in which shortages exist. If temporary wage differentials reflect the comparative scarcities of labour, the labour market mechanism would adjust wages and, in steady state, the equilibrium wage rates will be equal in all sectors of the economy. However, in the presence of economic or non-economic barriers to the mobility of labour, a shift in demand in one sector may result in persistent wage differentials among the affected sectors. Changes in relative wages paid in various industries, enterprises or occupations could indicate a long-term shortage. Economic barriers to mobility, such as high costs of relocation and retraining, restrictions on immigration or emigration or the existence of other institutional barriers could explain why market adjustments may be restricted and unable to clear the labour market.

PATH DEPENDENCE

The notion of path dependence could provide another interpretation of the inefficiency of the labour market mechanism. When employers find that there is a shortage in one occupation, they may try to restructure occupations and duties and make organizational changes to deal with the shortage. In that case path dependence becomes a relevant factor. When a change in demand shifts the equilibrium to a different level the path history plays a significant role because of the behaviour of employers.

JOB VACANCIES

The four concepts discussed above provide some explanations for the failure of labour markets to clear. Both short-term and long-term shortages can exist. A shift in demand, which is not accompanied by a subsequent shift in supply, could signal a temporary shortage. If demand shifts faster than supply can catch up, the shortage could last a long time. In addition, an increase in the typical length of time it takes to fill a vacancy could be evidence of a shortage.

In a steady state, vacancies and new hires would be equal. A theory of shortages (Abraham, 1983) suggests that the vacancy rate can be computed according to the equation:

$$VR = NHR * d_v \tag{2.2}$$

where NHR is the new hire rate, d_v is the average length of time that a vacancy remains open, and VR is the vacancy rate.

If vacancies begin to outpace the new hires, a shortage develops. Therefore we would want to measure vacancies, permanent and temporary new hires and other labour market indicators in order to identify shortages in various occupations and to understand the mechanism of a market disequilibrium.

Job vacancy surveys could help identify occupations in which shortages exist. Job vacancies, alone, would not be enough since the data would need to be interpreted in conjunction with other labour market indicators, such as the unemployment rate. For example, an occupation with high turnover and poor labour market information about openings or barriers to mobility could experience a high vacancy rate along with a high unemployment rate. A fuller analysis of labour market conditions would be required to understand the dynamics of the market for a particular occupation. Furthermore, data are too limited to be used to determine actual shortages, and surveys would not be of any help in providing statistically reliable information at a detailed level.

Although the growth of vacancies and new hires could be one of the best indicators of skill shortages, the problems discussed above make this measure insufficient. Therefore the unemployment rate has been used as a proxy for excess labour demand, and the importance of the relationship between unfilled vacancies and unemployment has been recognized. Efforts have been made to examine the condition of excess demand in the labour market in terms of vacancy and unemployment data (Dow and Dicks-Mireaux, 1958; Zaidi, 1970). The objective of these efforts has been to relate the statistics of unemployment and of unfilled vacancies to design indices measuring the pressure of labour demand. The results show that the data on unfilled vacancies can be successfully related to unemployment figures and meaningful indices can be constructed based on the relationship between those two measures. These indices can be used to reflect the low and high periods of excess labour demand.

In the absence of direct measures of job vacancies, indirect measures have been used. Solow (1964) suggested that help-wanted advertising could be a good proxy for job vacancies. There is evidence that help-wanted advertising is related to the unemployment rate, inversely correlated with changes in new hires and affected by the business cycle (Cohen and Solow, 1967, 1970). Help-wanted advertising is used more intensely as the business cycle recovery progresses; other recruitment methods, such as informal practices, recalls and direct applications, do not produce satisfactory results and workers become harder to locate. The model developed by Cohen and Solow (1967, 1970) did a credible job of explaining changes in help-wanted advertising. However, when total economy-wide new hires were used instead of manufacturing new hires, the results were different because firms in other industries may have more trouble recruiting workers than firms in manufacturing (Blanchard and Diamond, 1989).

There is some evidence of an upward bias of the help-wanted index used as a proxy for the job vacancy rate. The inference is that help-wanted ads placed in large metropolitan area newspapers are not representative of all vacancies. They are used to attract professional, urban, white-collar employees, service sector employees and some skilled workers. Unskilled workers in the manufacturing sector are recruited through other processes such as employment agencies. As a result, shifts in the occupational composition of employment away from blue-collar jobs and toward more heavily advertised white-collar jobs would cause an upward drift in the help-wanted index relative to vacancies.

Efforts have been made to identify and quantify the main reasons why the help-wanted index shifts upward relative to vacancies (Abraham, 1987; Siebert and Zaidi, 1994). In addition to the shifts in the occupational composition of employment previously discussed changes in affirmative action and equal opportunity employment laws, which required employers to advertise jobs more widely, would increase the level of help-wanted advertising relative to vacancies. However, the decline in newspaper competition due to mergers and bankruptcies and the increasing popularity of Internet job sites would cause a downward shift if only newspapers are measured.

The definition of the term 'new hires' and their identification depend on the context in which they are viewed. A good indicator of new hires should give the best insight into what is happening in the labour force. The number of hiring transactions versus the number of individuals, permanent new hires versus total new hires and job turnover versus occupational turnover are three relevant distinctions which could be used in the design and evaluation of an indicator. Cohen (1995) discusses these distinctions as well as the ways to refine new hire rates and develops a model to update new hire estimates that is based on the relationship between changes in employment and turnover measures. By definition, the relationship between new hires and the change in employment is given by:

$$NH = \Delta E + Z \qquad (2.3)$$

where *NH* is new hires, ΔE is change in employment and *Z* is computed according to the equation:

$$Z = quits + other\ separations + lay\text{-}offs - recalls \qquad (2.4)$$

The unemployment rate (*UR*) is introduced as a proxy for *Z*. Unemployment is one of the key variables in the theory of labour turnover (Hall, 1972) and it is related to the components of *Z*. Net lay-offs (lay-offs minus recalls) are positively correlated with the unemployment rate, since one expects more lay-offs in an economic downturn than in a business recovery. Quits are negatively correlated, since employees are reluctant to quit when unemployment is high. Other separations are not explainable by any simple proxy, since they include diverse factors such as leave for military duty, retirement, death and certain inter-company transfers. Furthermore, there are no available data on the individual components of *Z* and the purpose of the analysis is not to estimate the components of turnover.

According to the above, using the unemployment rate as a proxy for *Z* will probably suffice and the following equation could be used to determine new hires:

$$NHR = f(UR, \%E) \qquad (2.5)$$

where *NHR* is the new hire rate (*NH*/*E*), *UR* is the unemployment rate, and *%E* is the percentage change in employment ($\Delta E/E$).

The theory of shortages and the surveys of literature indicate a number of measures of skill shortages such as vacancies, permanent and temporary new hires and other labour market indicators. A model to explain job vacancies or new hires would use variables such as the unemployment rate and the rate of change of employment. Indirect measures of job vacancies or new hires such as help-wanted advertising could be used to explain some variations. In addition, wages paid to new hires and replacement demand are two factors suggested by the shortages theory. If departing workers cannot be replaced as soon as desired, vacancies can develop in specific occupations even when the total number of workers needed does not change. Increasing wages of new hires is one mechanism that can be used to attract new workers when shortages exist. Other measures of skill shortages could be the level of training and experience required for various occupations, government forecasts of future demand and immigrants admitted by occupation.

MEASURES OF LABOUR SHORTAGES

All measures have advantages and disadvantages. Restrictions are always imposed by the labour market conditions, the idiosyncrasies of specific occupations and the availability and reliability of the data. However, using the measure suggested by the theory and the literature will probably suffice. The six indicators discussed below are among those that are theoretically justified and their choice and use could provide a solution to the problem of identifying and understanding skill shortages.

In general a low unemployment rate suggests a skill shortage. However, a high level of unemployment does not necessarily guarantee there is not a skill shortage. Job vacancies could exist even with an unemployment rate significantly above zero. Some additional drawbacks to the measure are those associated with the correctness of occupational classification, frictional unemployment and variations across occupations because of differences in search time unrelated to skill shortages, the correspondence between theoretical and available official measures, and so on. Although these factors may play a role, the unemployment rate is one of the principal explanatory variables suggested by the theory of shortages. In addition, it is the most direct measure of skill shortage available.

Another principal explanatory variable suggested by the theory of skill shortages is the rate of growth of employment. It reflects the trend in demand for workers in particular occupations. A skill shortage is more likely to occur if demand is increasing than if it remains constant or declines. The disadvantages of the measure are those associated with the correctness of occupational classifications and the relationship between employment changes and changes in demand for workers.

Rapidly rising wages are consistent with a skill shortage since wages will be bid up when demand exceeds supply. Therefore the rate of change in wages could be a measure of skill shortages. This indicator reflects both demand and the supply of workers and, together with the unemployment rate, provides more reliable information about the market conditions. The availability and the reliability of data are among the disadvantages of this measure. Data may not include changes in benefits or working conditions as well as changes in self-employed workers' wages, and may exclude commissions or other pay received irregularly. In addition, wages may change for reasons other than fluctuations in demand and supply.

Employers may have difficulty filling positions requiring high levels of education, training or experience. Therefore the level of training requirements could play a significant role in the determination of supply of various occupations.

Government forecasts of future demand could be used as an additional measure of shortages. Projected changes in employment provide a longer-term view of the conditions in the labour market and a better interpretation of the growth in demand for various occupations. The presumption is that the occupations with the highest projected occupational growth are the most likely to have a skill shortage.

Finally, immigrants admitted by occupation as a percentage of the labour force in an occupation could be used as another measure of skill shortages. A large number of labour certifications is a positive indicator of shortages. However, labour certifications do not necessarily reflect the labour market conditions, since a legal process like this may generate different results than would an economic analysis, and the regulations used may not always identify national shortages or surpluses.

The latter two indicators were available in Cohen's (1995) study in the United States but are rarely available in other countries at the occupational level.

Notes:

1. The material in this chapter largely draws on the authors' previous work (Siebert and Zaidi, 1994; Cohen, 1995; Cohen and Zaidi, 1998). Some material in this chapter is used with the permission of the University of Michigan Press © by the University of Michigan, 1995.
2. For an excellent discussion of instances of market failures resulting in a lack of the right kind of skills, see Booth and Snower (1996).
3. For a concise review of labor market models, see Bosworth and Warren (1992).

REFERENCES

Abraham, Katharine G. (1983), 'Structural/Frictional vs. Deficient Demand Unemployment: Some New Evidence', *American Economic Review*, **73** (4), 708–24.

Abraham, Katharine G. (1987), 'Help-wanted Advertising, Job Vacancies and Unemployment', *Brookings Papers on Economic Activity*, **1**, 207–48.

Akerlof, George and J. Yellen (1986), *Efficiency Wage Models of the Labor Market*, Cambridge, MA: Cambridge University Press.

Arrow, Kenneth J. and W. Capron (1959), 'Dynamic Shortages and Price Rises: The Engineer–Scientist Case', *Quarterly Journal of Economics*, **73** (2), 292–308.

Blanchard, Olivier J. and P. Diamond (1989), 'The Beveridge Curve', *Brookings Papers on Economics Activity*, **1**, 1–76.

Blank, David M. and G. Stigler (1957), *The Demand and Supply of Scientific Personnel*, New York: National Bureau of Economic Research.

Booth, Alison and D. Snower (eds) (1996), *Acquiring Skills: Market Failures, Their Symptoms and Policy Responses*, Cambridge, MA: Cambridge University Press.

Bosworth, Derek and P. Warren (1992), 'Modeling Skill Shortages', in Derek Bosworth, P. Dutton and J. Lewis (eds), *Skill Shortages: Causes and Consequences*, Aldershot: Ashgate Publishing.

Cohen, Malcolm S. (1995), *Labor Shortages as America Approaches the Twenty-first Century*, Ann Arbor, MI: University of Michigan Press.

Cohen, Malcolm S. and R. Solow (1967), 'The Behavior of Help-Wanted Advertising', *Review of Economics and Statistics*, **49** (1), 108–10.

Cohen, Malcolm S. and R. Solow (1970), 'The Behavior of Help-Wanted Advertising: A Reply', *Review of Economics and Statistics*, **52** (4), 442–3.

Cohen, Malcolm S. and M. Zaidi (1998), 'Labor Shortages, Pay and Training in NAFTA Countries', *North American Journal of Economics and Finance*, **9** (1), 89-103.

Dow, J.C.R. and L. Dicks-Mireaux (1958) 'The Excess Demand for Labour: A Study of Conditions in Great Britain, 1946–56', *Oxford Economic Papers*, **10** (1), 1–33.

Gallaway, Lowell E. (1963), 'Labor Mobility, Resource Allocation and Structural Unemployment', *American Economic Review*, **53** (4), 694–717.

Hall, Robert (1972), 'Turnover in the Labor Force', *Brookings Papers on Economic Activities*, **3**, 709–56.

Lindbeck, Assar and D. Snower (1988), *The Insider-Outsider Theory of Employment and Unemployment*, Cambridge, MA: MIT Press.

Lindbeck, Assar and D. Snower (2001), 'Insiders versus Outsiders', *Journal of Economic Perspectives*, **15** (1), 165–88.

Muysken, J. (ed.) (1994), *Measurement and Analysis of Job Vacancies: An International Comparison*, Aldershot: Avebury Publishing.

Padoa-Schioppa, Fiorella (ed.) (1991), *Mismatch and Labour Mobility*, Cambridge, MA: Cambridge University Press.

Siebert, C.D. and M. Zaidi (1994), 'Measures of Excess Demand and Unemployment in Canada and the United States', *Relations Industrielles*, **49** (3), 503–26.

Solow, Robert M. (1964), 'The Nature and Sources of Unemployment in the United States', *Wicksell Lectures*, Stockholm: Almquist and Wicksell.

Solow, Robert M. (1990), *The Labor Market as a Social Institution*, Cambridge, MA: Basil Blackwell.

Trutko, John W., B. Barnow, A. Chasanov and A. Pande (1991), *Labor Shortage Case Studies*, Washington, DC: US Department of Labor, Employment and Training Administration.

Zaidi, Mahmood A. (1969), 'Structural Unemployment, Labor Market Efficiency and the Intrafactor Allocation Mechanism in the United States and Canada', *Southern Economic Journal*, **35** (3), 205–13.

Zaidi, Mahmood A. (1970), 'Unemployment, Vacancies and Conditions of Excess Demand for Labor in Canada', *Applied Economics*, **2** (2), 101–12.

3. Globalization and skill shortages

Shortages of skilled workers were among the most challenging obstacles faced by businesses in the 1990s. As G. Pascal Zachary (2000), writing in the *Wall Street Journal*, observed, 'with skilled workers in high demand, employers are hunting them down – no matter where they live'.

Given the emergence of global markets and global production it is important that studies of occupational skill shortages be global in scope. As pointed out by Jeffrey Sachs (1997), 'for the first time in history, almost all of the world's people are bound together in a global capitalist system. This momentous development forces us to think anew about the world economy'. Countries seeking qualified workers are drawing from a worldwide talent pool instead of a national labour force, forcing one to think in terms of 'brain circulation' rather than 'brain drain'.[1] Evidence of this phenomenon is found in the immigration policies of countries experiencing worker shortages in certain fields: Canada's immigration policy is already focused on accepting workers with special skills; Australia's immigration policy is aimed at easing the immigration of highly skilled workers; Taiwanese engineers leave Silicon Valley to start businesses at home but keep links with businesses in the United States; Singapore's government provides tax incentives to companies that bring in needed talent from other countries; and the United States high-tech industry increasingly draws on foreign talent. As national economies are becoming deeply intertwined with one another and the global economy is becoming more closely integrated, it becomes increasingly important to study issues such as labour market skill shortages in a global context (Cohen and Zaidi, 2000). There is much debate about globalization being good or bad for jobs, incomes, labor standards, environment and national sovereignty (Rodrik, 1997). Suffice here to say that irrespective of how one feels about globalization, the shifts toward integrated and interdependent global economy is likely to be continuous, and in the long run, the only way the rich countries are likely to stay rich and the emerging economies are going to become richer is to be more productive.

This chapter addresses the forces which drive globalization and make economies interdependent. The following chapter shows that skill shortages are worldwide by discussing a number of studies concerning skill shortages conducted in many of the countries included in the present study.

GLOBALIZATION AND TRADE

The volume of United States trade with the 18 other countries included in this study, as well as other parts of the world, is described in Tables 3.1 and 3.2. These tables show the share of imports or exports of total trade by the United States with other countries.[2] Table 3.1 shows total United States commodity trade (exports plus imports) with different regions and selected countries.

Table 3.1 Total United States trade 1991–99 (millions of dollars)

	1991	1999	% Change
European Union	201 447	347 014	72.27
Western Hemisphere	302 113	657 582	123.62
NAFTA[a]	240 621	561 941	133.54
South America	42 023	72 737	73.09
Asia	340 836	599 423	75.89
Japan	139 636	188 330	34.87
Republic of Korea	32 523	54 137	66.46
Taiwan	36 205	54 335	50.08
China	25 247	94 899	275.88
ASEAN[b]	49 749	117 599	136.38
Australia and Oceania	15 134	21 544	42.35
Africa	22 822	26 870	17.74

Notes: a. North American Free Trade Agreement
b. Association of South East Asian Nations

Source: US Department of Commerce, Bureau of Economic Analysis, Balance of Payments Division (2000).

Table 3.2 shows United States commodity trade in 1999 with the 18 countries included in this study. 'Total Trade' is the sum of exports and imports with the United States in 1999. 'Share of Total Trade' indicates total trade volume of each country expressed as a percentage of total United States trade in 1999.

Table 3.2 United States trade with selected countries, 1999 (millions of dollars)

	Rank by Share	Export	Import	Total Trade	Share of Total Trade %
Canada	1	163 913	198 324	362 237	21.06
Mexico	2	87 044	109 706	196 750	11.44
Japan	3	57 484	131 404	188 888	10.98
Germany	4	26 789	55 094	81 883	4.76
United Kingdom	5	38 338	39 191	77 529	4.51
Republic of Korea	6	22 954	31 262	54 216	3.15
France	7	18 838	25 910	44 748	2.60
Singapore	8	16 246	18 188	34 434	2.00
Italy	9	10 094	22 438	32 532	1.89
Belgium	10	12 385	9 208	21 593	1.26
Australia	11	11 811	5 290	17 101	0.99
Sweden	12	4 239	8 111	12 350	0.72
Spain	13	6 123	5 055	11 178	0.65
Chile	14	3 079	2 936	6 015	0.35
Austria	15	2 588	2 910	5 498	0.32
Denmark	16	1 719	2 825	4 544	0.26
Portugal	17	1 091	1 357	2 448	0.14
Greece	18	994	571	1 565	0.09

Source: US Department of Commerce, International Trade Administration (2001).

According to the United Nations Conference of Trade and Development (1999), foreign direct investment (FDI) flows have experienced explosive growth since the 1980s. As Table 3.3 shows, the annual growth rate of FDI inflows and outflows increased respectively from 24.3 per cent and 27.3 per cent between 1986 and 1990, to 38.7 per cent and 36.6 per cent in 1998. Inflows and outflows of United States direct investment in 1999 for the 18 countries are described in Table 3.4. Each country is ranked by share of trade and capital outflows and inflows of investments to show the extent of United States involvement in the international economy.

Table 3.3 Annual growth rate of foreign direct investment (FDI) 1986–98

	Annual Growth Rate (%)				
	1986–90	1991–95	1996	1997	1998
FDI inflows	24.3	19.6	9.1	29.4	38.7
FDI outflows	27.3	15.9	5.9	25.1	36.6

Source: United Nations Conference of Trade and Development (1999).

Table 3.4 Direct investment position for 1999 (millions of dollars)

Countries Ranked by Capital Outflow	US Direct Investment Abroad (Capital Outflows)	Countries Ranked by Capital Inflow	FDI in the US (Capital Inflows)
Canada	111 707	United Kingdom	183 145
Germany	49 617	Japan	148 947
Japan	47 786	Germany	111 138
France	39 984	Canada	79 716
Mexico	34 625	France	77 622
Australia	33 662	Sweden	17 904
Singapore	24 781	Belgium	11 448
United Kingdom	21 070	Australia	10 818
Italy	17 595	Italy	4 982
Belgium	17 285	Denmark	4 959
Spain	12 456	Mexico	3 162
Chile	9 886	Spain	2 629
Sweden	9 595	Austria	2 483
Republic of Korea	8 749	Republic of Korea	1 520
Denmark	3 887	Singapore	1 049
Austria	3 696	Greece	159
Portugal	1 478	Portugal	n.a.
Greece	602	Chile	n.a.

Source: US Department of Commerce, Bureau of Economic Analysis (2000).

Both the sharp increase in trade and the growth of FDI suggest that the world economy is becoming much more interdependent. The discussion now turns to the globalization of markets and the globalization of production.

GLOBALIZATION OF MARKETS

Two key factors have contributed to the increasing globalization of markets: (1) the decline in barriers to trade and investment, and (2) the role of technological change.

The decline in trade barriers (that is, average tariff rates for manufactured goods) under the Uruguay agreement has been close to 4 per cent (Wooldridge, 1995). This trend, combined with weakening restrictions on capital inflows and outflows, has enabled firms to view the world as a single marketplace and has facilitated the globalization of production. The global popularity of products such as Coca-Cola, Sony Walkman, Levi's jeans, and McDonalds is a testament to the worldwide convergence of tastes and preferences made possible by increased access to foreign markets.

The rate of decline in the cost of a new technology is a good gauge of the pace of technological change. Technological advances accompanied by a substantial decline in the cost of new technology in communications, information processing and transportation, as well as the emergence of the Internet and World Wide Web, have enabled firms to coordinate worldwide operations to meet demands of worldwide customers. According to Pam Woodall (2000), 'over the past three decades, the real price of computer processing has fallen by 99.999% – an average decline of 35% a year'. In addition to the decline in costs, Woodall discusses how the pervasiveness of information technologies (IT) has facilitated increasing access to information, thus making markets function more efficiently. She points out that computers and the Internet have intimate links to globalization by helping to globalize production and capital markets and by helping to speed up innovations and designs of new products. There seems to be a consensus that productivity in the sector producing IT goods has surged. However, there is disagreement about the effect of IT on the rest of the economy (Jorgenson, 2001).

GLOBALIZATION OF PRODUCTION

Moving production of goods out of the country allows companies to take advantage of differences in production costs, as well as factors such as labour, land, capital and energy. For example, according to Robert Reich (1991), less than 40 per cent of the cost of a General Motors Pontiac Lemans comes from services or parts manufactured in the United States, even though it is an 'American-made' product. In essence, Reich says that it does not make much sense to speak of 'American', 'German' or 'Japanese' products because many products are actually globally produced.

Reich addresses the question of what makes a company 'American'. He considers two hypothetical companies (see Table 3.5) and asks which firm is the 'American' company. Additionally, he questions which company is more important for United States economic welfare. One company, ABC Computers, is headquartered in San Francisco. All of its managers, directors and stockholders are United States citizens but most of the other employees are from the Republic of Korea. Many of its products are exported to the United States. The other company, XYZ Computers, is headquartered in Germany. All of its managers, directors and stockholders are German citizens but most of the other employees are Californians. Many of its products are exported to Germany.

Which firm is the 'American' company? Reich concludes that XYZ Computers is more important to the United States economic welfare than the ABC Computers from a competitiveness point of view. In other words, even though the headquarters of the hypothetical company is in Germany and even though the managers and directors are German, design and manufacturing takes place in California by American workers. Reich defines 'American competitiveness' as the capacity of United States workers to add value to the global economy. The policy implication of this viewpoint is that countries must provide opportunities and jobs for their workers in order to maintain and increase the economic well-being of their citizens. If countries want to maintain their competitive position, they must focus on productivity.

There is widespread consensus in the economic arena that trade liberalization generates aggregate net benefits (Arndt, 2000). Additionally, FDI is more than mere capital. As was pointed out recently ('The Cutting Edge', 2001), 'it is a uniquely potent bundle of capital, contacts and managerial and technological knowledge'. However, there are short-run adjustment costs associated with trade liberalization. FDI, like international trade, has an impact on the demand for skilled workers. A recent study on this subject (Driffield and Taylor, 2000) found that one of the impacts of

FDI was to increase the use of relatively more skilled labour in the host country. There is also some evidence of deterioration in the demand for less skilled workers (Greenaway and Nelson, 2000).

Table 3.5 What makes a company 'American?'

ABC Computers	XYZ Computers
a) HQ = San Francisco	a) HQ = Germany
b) Managers, directors and stockholders are US citizens.	b) Managers, directors and stockholders are German citizens
c) Most of the other employees are from the Republic of Korea because: The firm conducts its product design and manufacturing in the Republic of Korea	c) Most of the other employees are Californians because: The firm conducts its product design and manufacturing in California
d) Many of these computers are exported to the US	d) Many of these computers are exported to Germany

Source: Adapted from Robert B. Reich, 'Who is Us?' 1990.

Job-related immigration is now part and parcel of globalization (Stalker, 2000). In a fairly large survey of the literature a recent study concluded that immigration had a very small effect on wages and unemployment (Gaston and Nelson, 2000). For example, two studies (Card, 1990; Friedberg, 1996) examining the impact of large immigration shocks reached similar conclusions. The first study dealt with the impact of the Mariel boatlift resulting in an increase of about 7 per cent in the Miami labour force, and the second one looked at the impact of Russian Jewish immigration resulting in an increase of 14 per cent of the Israeli labour force.

The impact of immigration on labour market outcomes (for example, impact on employment and earnings of the native-born population) is somewhat controversial. Since immigration has economic, political and social implications, controversy on this subject is understandable.

In this chapter the interrelationship of global markets and their impact on skill shortages were discussed. In the next chapter anecdotal information about skill shortages in different countries in our study is provided.

1. The term 'brain circulation' was coined by Alan Findlay of the University of Dundee and is quoted by G. Pascal Zachary (2000).
2. It is important to note here that for many years the volume of world trade has been growing faster than the volume of world output. See World Trade Organization (2000), and Brewer and Boyd (2000).

REFERENCES

Arndt, Sven (2000), 'The United States In The World Trading System', in Thomas L. Brewer and G. Boyd (eds), *Globalizing America: The USA in World Integration*, Cheltenham: Edward Elgar.

Brewer, Thomas L. and G. Boyd (eds) (2000), *Globalizing America: The USA in World Integration*, Cheltenham: Edward Elgar.

Card, David (1990), 'The Impact of the Mariel Boatlift On the Miami Labor Market', *Industrial and Labor Relations Review*, **43** (2), 245–57.

Cohen, Malcolm S. and M. Zaidi (2000), 'Global Skill Shortages', *Economic Outlook for 2001*, Department of Economics, Ann Arbor, MI: University of Michigan, 206-26.

'The Cutting Edge' (2001), *The Economist*, **358** (8210), 80.

Driffield, Nigel and K. Taylor (2000), 'FDI and the Labour Market: A Review of the Evidence and Policy Implications', *Oxford Review of Economic Policy*, **16** (3), 90–103.

Friedberg, Rachel (1996), 'The Impact of Mass Migration On the Israeli Labor Market', *Brown University Department of Economics Working Paper*, No. 96/28, mimeograph.

Gaston, Noel and D. Nelson (2000), 'The Employment and Wage Effects of Immigration: Perspectives From Labor Trade Economics', Murphy Institute of Political Economy, mimeograph.

Greenaway, David and D. Nelson (2000), 'The Assessment: Globalization and Labour- Market Adjustment', *Oxford Review of Economic Policy*, **16** (3), 1–11.

Jorgenson, Dale W. (2001), 'Information Technology and the US Economy', *American Economic Review*, **91**, (1), 1–32.

Reich, Robert B. (1990), 'Who is Us?', *Harvard Business Review*, **68** (1), 53–64.

Reich, Robert B. (1991), *The Work of Nations: Preparing Ourselves for 21st Century Capitalism*, New York: Alfred A. Knopf.

Rodrik, Dani (1997), *Has Globalization Gone Too Far?*, Washington, DC: Institute for International Economics.

Sachs, Jeffrey (1997), 'Nature, Nurture and Growth', *The Economist*, **343** (8021), 19–22.

Stalker, Peter (2000), *Workers Without Frontiers: The Impact of Globalization on International Migration*, Geneva: International Labour Organization.

United Nations Conference of Trade and Development (1999), *World Economic Report, United Nations; World Investment Report.*

US Department of Commerce, Bureau of Economic Analysis, Balance of Payments Division (2000), *Total US Trade*, 27 July.

US Department of Commerce, Bureau of Economic Analysis (2000), http://www.bea.doc.gov/bea/di1.htm, 'US Direct Investment Abroad and Balance of Payments', 2 August.

US Department of Commerce, International Trade Administration (2001), Office of Trade and Economic Analysis, http://www.ita.doc.gov/statistics.html, June.

Woodall, Pam (2000), 'The New Economy: Elementary My Dear Watson', *The Economist*, **356** (8189), S7–S11.

Wooldridge, Adrian (1995), 'Who Wants To Be A Giant?', *The Economist*, **335** (7920), SS3–4.

World Trade Organization (2000), *International Trade Trends and Statistics,1999*, US Department of Commerce, International Trade Administration, 27 July.

Zachary, G. Pascal (2000), 'The Global Battle – People Who Need People: With Skilled Workers in High Demand, Employers Are Hunting Them Down – No Matter Where They Live', *Wall Street Journal*, 25 September, R8.

4. Skill shortage studies in selected countries

This chapter begins by summarizing some empirical studies on labour shortages in selected countries and regions. Most of the studies reported here relate to the period from 1995 to 1998, which corresponds to the period when the labour shortage indicators in this book were developed. These indicators are discussed in Chapter 5.

AUSTRALIA

According to the Australian Department of Employment (1998), skill shortages were evident in three broad occupational areas: professional occupations, which include mining engineers, selected computing professionals, registered nurses and health professionals; skilled trades, including toolmakers, boilermakers, sheet metal workers, chefs, pastry cooks and hairdressers; and service occupations such as childcare coordinators.

Australia was experiencing a skills transformation as businesses rapidly changed their practices and developed new products using information technology. The rapid spread of new technology was shaping Australia's future occupational structure and the skill needs for most industries and occupations. A study in 1998 found that skill shortages in the information technology and telecommunication (IT&T) industries were being seen increasingly as a key constraint to the growth and competitiveness of industry in Australia and to the emerging information economy (*Skill Shortage in Australia's IT&T Industry*, 1998). Evidence suggested that skill shortages existed for IT&T professionals with experience in certain specializations. In the long term, it would be necessary to ensure that there is an adequate supply of appropriately qualified graduates and other IT&T skilled workers to meet growth in IT&T occupations. An industry publication reported that there were worsening skills shortages in technology (Guth et al., 1998). A shortfall of between 20 000 and 25 000 skilled staff existed in the Australian technology industry.

BELGIUM

While unemployment in Belgium was slowly declining, developments in the labour market were uneven. In particular there were strong regional differences with unemployment levels in Wallonia and Brussels being twice as high as those in Flanders. High labour costs remained a problem in all regions. Business efforts to neutralize high labour costs through labour saving and capital-intensive investment had increased productivity. Belgium had eased tax rules to make it easier for businesses to offer employees stock options. In spite of these efforts, shortages of technical professionals remained (US Department of Commerce, 1999). Some people having difficulty finding employment due to lack of the proper skills needed by the current labour market were retraining as IT professionals (Ewing and Dawly, 1999).

CANADA

The Canadian economy had been employing an increasing number of knowledge workers in recent years. Gingras and Roy (1998) examined microeconomic data and found that there was an increased frequency of specific labour shortages in certain sectors and occupations, such as human resource managers, systems analysts and computer programmers, machinists and tool and die workers.

High-tech companies were facing skill shortages. The debate was whether or not the so-called 'brain drain' of talent out of Canada was fact or fiction. It was the quality of the people moving south (to the United States), not the quantity, that was hurting Canada's labour market. Canada's taxes were cited as a major factor in the migration of skilled workers (DeCloet, 1999).

Without the required talent, some industries were predicting a bleak future. In some cases, the numbers were staggering. The auto manufacturing industry was predicting a need for between 10 000 and 14 000 skilled workers in the upcoming five to ten years, auto parts makers needed about 15 000 additional workers by 2006, and the Canadian Trucking Alliance wanted 50 000 new drivers immediately (Pappone, 2000). According to the *Electronics Communicator*, 'without 18,000 workers, Canada risks losing a major portion of its global industry to other countries' ('SMC and Partners Make Modest Progress in Addressing Microelectronics Skills Shortage', 2000).

CHILE

A study carried out by the University of Chile revealed that education, especially technical training, was a problem in Chile. The rapid advance of technology made this a particularly serious deficiency, and high-tech firms in Chile were increasingly concerned that they would soon run up against a shortage of skilled labour. In addition these firms usually wanted their employees to be proficient in English; this requirement significantly increased their recruitment difficulties (Chilean American Chamber of Commerce, 2001).

EUROPE

The latest European benchmarking survey from PricewaterhouseCoopers (PWC) revealed that the growth of high-tech start-up companies in Europe was being stifled by the shortage of highly skilled staff. Indeed the report claimed that such a shortage had halved the growth of companies in this sector. Keith Evans of PWC states, 'The growth rate for the last year was 34.5 per cent, which is ten per cent above the year before. But everyone said that they would have grown much more quickly if they'd had more skilled staff. Growth rates could have been as high as 60 to 70 per cent' (Europemedia.net, 2000). Of the 289 companies questioned, more than 70 per cent said they were having severe difficulties recruiting staff with key skills and experience. Most of these companies believed the resources would worsen in the next few years. European Commission estimates that the 'shortage of IT specialists in Western Europe ... could reach 1.6 million unless necessary training and adaption initiatives are undertaken' (European Commission, 2000). Many firms were looking outside of the EU to countries such as India and Sri Lanka to find programmers and other skilled workers (Europemedia.net, 2000).

GERMANY

The need for software engineers was being fuelled by technology development around the world and the globalization of the electric industry. With United States visa quotas running out quickly each year, international recruitment efforts were increasing the flow of Indian software engineers to countries other than the United States. Germany had launched a programme similar to the United States H-1B visa programme to ease the immigration of certain kinds of workers and promote Germany as a preferred destination for foreign engineers seeking employment (Watson, 2001).

Nicola Düll (1998) argues that although Germany had a high unemployment rate, it had labour shortages within very specific labour market segments. This could be overcome if migrants had the right skills profile. Widely hailed as the answer to Germany's high-tech worker shortage, the so-called 'green card initiative' had been in place then for over two months. The programme was designed to ease the labour shortage by bringing as many as 20 000 highly skilled foreign employees to work both in start-ups and in large multinational corporations.

Expansion of Germany's software industry was being seriously slowed by a lack of specialist personnel, according to a German engineering industry association, *Verband Deutscher Maschinen-und Anlagenbau e.v.* (VDMA). Karl Gosejacob, chairman of the VDMA's software industry section, said 86 per cent of companies surveyed planned to recruit more software personnel in the year ahead. But companies believed they would be able to recruit only 39 per cent of the IT personnel they needed. Gosejacob had been quoted as saying that despite the generally positive trend in the German software industry, the shortage of specialist personnel was 'considerably slowing possible growth' ('Manpower Shortage Slows Growth', 2000).

GREECE

Greece was also experiencing skill shortages in certain occupations. In 1995, public investment in education in Greece was the lowest in the EU and expenditure on active employment policies was similarly inadequate. This had led to a shortage of skills, particularly in specialized areas (*The European Social Fund, an Overview of the Programming Period, 1994–99*, 1998).

JAPAN

Japan was facing a rapidly aging population and a sharply declining birth rate. There was a risk that 'further [economic] growth will run out of steam in the absence of new sources of labour...the drop in the number of skilled technicians was so severe that it crimps overall economic growth' (Dawson, 1999).

Due to rapid economic growth and the continued labour shortage in small-scale industries, the number of migrant workers increased significantly during the 1980s. The small-scale industries, along with the Chambers of Commerce and Industry, asked the government to import migrant workers to help alleviate the labour shortage. In order to deal with the increasing number of foreign workers, the revised Immigration Act was agreed upon in the Diet in December 1989, and came into effect in June 1990. The descendants of Japanese abroad were given new work permits to fill the labour shortage, and the number of migrant workers eventually increased to 180 000 as of 1996 (Inagami, 1998).

There was concern that the drop in the number of able-bodied manual labourers and highly skilled technicians in the early next century could be so severe that it would crimp overall economic growth rates. According to Makoto Nomuva, Chief Economist at Sumitomo Life Research Institute, Japan had to lower barriers to labour inflow. As a recent survey pointed out, 'like it or not, Japan may be forced to accommodate foreigners and unfamiliar cultures and habits to prosper in the coming decades' (Dawson, 1999).

PORTUGAL

Portugal was successful in attracting investment in low- or medium-tech manufacturing operations, such as the automotive and electronics industries. Labour costs were low in Portugal and the workforce had been reliable, educated and flexible. However, there had been a low penetration of PCs and a lack of knowledge, and 'most managers didn't know much about the Internet or email' (Roberts, 1999/2000).

REPUBLIC OF KOREA

The Republic of Korea used to be a labour exporting country, but before the Asian financial crisis of 1997 it was also recruiting foreign labour to fill the gap in skill shortages. The labour shortage problem was more serious with labour-intensive industries such as clothing, small- and medium-sized industries and the construction industry. The Korean labour market had been near full employment since the mid-1980s. Unemployment rates had been around 2.5 per cent. In 1995, the unemployment rate was only 2 per cent. With this tight labour market, some industries had difficulties in finding Korean workers and foreign workers trickled into the country.

According to one study (Jeong, 1996) the Korean machine tool industry experienced skill shortages both on quantitative and qualitative grounds.

SINGAPORE

A study on the labour market policies in Asian countries by Takeshi Inagami (1998) pointed out that there was a serious quantitative labour shortage problem in Singapore. The Ministry of Trade and Industry reported that in order for Singapore to remain competitive it had to address various limitations. Some of the key economic strategies involved the continual upgrading of the labour force, prompting new economic activities in the manufacturing and service sectors, restructuring the domestic sector and promoting research and development. To meet this economic plan and direction the demand for various skills and qualifications in the banking, finance, accounting and investment management sectors, for example, prompted the government of Singapore to focus on achieving a higher level of education for Singaporeans. Meanwhile, more and more Singaporeans held white-collar jobs, so many blue-collar jobs had to rely heavily on imported workers from neighbouring countries.

Bloomberg (2000) reported that Singapore planned to attract 1000 foreign employees for its telecommunications, IT and computer industries within a year. The Infocomm Development Authority of Singapore (2000) (IDA) added that shortages in information communication talents affected many high-growth sectors in Singapore. IDA expected demand for employees in these industries to grow at an average annual rate of 10 per cent, or 10 000 employees, in the upcoming two years.

UNITED STATES

The United States economy in the 1990s was in the midst of the longest expansion in the nation's history. Non-farm payroll employment increased by nearly 21 million workers during the decade. There was strong employment growth mid-decade in the technology and service sector (Hatch and Clinton, 2000). The private service-producing industry accounted for nearly 90 per cent of job growth in the 1990s. Veneri (1999) analysed the employment trends of 68 occupations and found seven of the 68 occupations had tight labour markets: management analysts, special education teachers, dental hygienists, marketing, advertising and public relations managers, aeroplane pilots and navigators, purchasing agents and buyers, and mechanical engineers.

According to *The Beige Book*, a publication by the Federal Reserve Board, 'There were more frequent reports of intensifying wage pressures as shortages of workers persisted in all Districts' (US Federal Reserve Board, 2000). This point perhaps can be illustrated by a survey of job openings carried out by the Minnesota Research Department of Economic Security, Research and Planning Branch (see Table 4.1). Many businesses surveyed considered securing workers a serious challenge for 2000. Many companies were still looking for skilled workers. These jobs were usually in high-skill and high-wage groups that required specialized training and post-secondary education.

Fiorino (2000) pointed out that there was a shortage of critical skills needed to repair increasingly sophisticated aircraft among airframe and power plant mechanics. One publication described the automotive industry as 'employee starved' (Sherefkin, 2000). There was a shortage of workers at all levels in the auto industry. In the telecom industry, companies were struggling to fill both managerial and technical positions. On the managerial side, it had been a challenge for companies to find 'top-notch' sales managers, while on the technical side, they simply could not find enough people (Richter, 2000). There was also a serious shortage of nurses, according to *Health Care Strategic Management* ('Hospitals May Help Relieve Nurse Shortage', 2000).

UNITED KINGDOM

Some of the best studies on shortages, both on theoretical and empirical grounds, have been carried out in the United Kingdom. Bosworth, Dutton and Lewis (1992) identified some of the problems associated with measuring and isolating skill shortages as well as the likely causes and consequences of those shortages. The articles addressed a wide variety of topics such as the relationship between skill shortages and economic prosperity, the role of technological innovation, the use of skill shortage surveys and the response of trade unions to labour shortages.

Bosworth (1993) attempted to define the probability that an establishment will report a skill shortage and, for those that do, the intensity of that shortage. He found evidence that skill shortages were less intense and less likely in establishments where an internal labour market existed, for example, large companies with offices in many locations. He also found that occupations associated with widespread skill shortages were not the occupations where shortages were most intense. According to another researcher, a recent survey by the UK's 70 national training organizations reported that 'The most severe skill shortages exist in technical occupations and sectors reliant on information technology or management skills' (Crequer, 1999). Due to this high demand for technology professionals

Table 4.1 Job openings by occupation group in the Twin Cities of Minnesota, April–June 2000

Major Occupation Groups	Job Vacancy Rate (%)
Healthcare support	14.00
Community and social services	10.20
Personal care and service	9.10
Construction and extraction	8.60
Healthcare practitioners and technical	6.10
Food preparation and serving	6.00
Computer and mathematical	5.40
Building and grounds cleaning and maintenance	5.40
Transportation and material moving	4.40
Installation, maintenance and repair	3.90
Farming, fishing and forestry	3.80
Sales and related	3.70
Production	3.60
Architecture and engineering	3.20
Protective service	2.90
Business and financial operations	2.80
Life, physical and social science	2.70
Art, design, entertainment, media	2.70
Education, training and library	2.30
Office and administration support	2.00
Management	1.80
Legal	1.00
All occupations	4.00

Source: Minnesota Department of Economic Security Research & Planning Branch (2000).

there was a sharp increase in their earnings. For example, a web-site specialist with one or two years of experience could earn up to $64 000 a year, a 20 per cent increase over the going rate 12 months prior. Pay for mid-level systems architects had been rising 10–12 per cent a year, according to human resources consultant Towers Perrin (Ewing and Dawly 1999).

SUMMARY

This chapter suggests that skill shortages existed in many countries in this sample during 1995–98. Also, labour shortages in certain occupations have been recognized as a problem in times of expansion as well as contraction. They have been found to create 'bottlenecks' and have an impact on the economic performance of companies, regions and countries (Lynch, 2000). Generally, concerns about labour shortages increase when rapid economic growth has been sustained for a number of years. In the initial period of recovery following a downturn, labour demand can be met by slack labour. After the slack labour becomes employed, shortages can emerge as a problem.

The economic cycle does not have the same effect on all occupations. Many variables determine whether shortages will actually occur in a given occupation (Abraham, 1991). Skill shortages do not have to be country-wide in scope; they can exist in a region of a country, in an industry or even a sub-specialty of an occupation. Skill shortages may even exist when the unemployment rate is very high.

Given that many companies are experiencing skill shortages, two questions arise: What options do companies have to deal with labour shortages in the short and long run? How have the firms been coping with labour shortages during the last few years? Chapter 7 discusses these two questions.

REFERENCES

Abraham, Katharine G. (1991), 'Mismatch and Labor Mobility: Some Final Remarks', in Fiorella Padoa-Schioppa (ed.), *Mismatch and Labor Mobility*, Cambridge, MA: Cambridge University Press.

'Asian Migration Yearbook: Country Report in Japan' (1998), *Migration Forum in Asia Network*, http://migrantnet.pair.com/resources.html#2.

Australia Department of Employment, Education, Training and Youth Affairs, Skills Analysis and Research Branch and Labor Economics Offices (1998), *Skills in Australia: Trends and Shortages*, Analytical Series: No. 98/5.

Bloomberg (2000), 'Singapore to Lure 1,000 Infocomm Staff From Region', http://www.niit.com/Asean/press82.htm, 28 August.

Bosworth, Derek (1993), 'Skill Shortages in Britain', *Scottish Journal of Political Economy*, **40** (3), 241–71.

Bosworth, Derek, P. Dutton and J. Lewis (eds) (1992), *Skill Shortages: Causes and Consequences*, Aldershot: Ashgate Publishing.

Brownlee, Patrick and C. Mitchell (eds) (1997), *Migration Issues in the Asia Pacific*, Asia Pacific Migration Research Network (APMRN), http://www.unesco.org/most/apmrnw12.htm.

Chilean American Chamber of Commerce, (2001), 'The Outlook for 2001', http://www.amchamchile.cl/publicat/journal/rep1.htm.

Crequer, Ngaio (1999), 'Skills Shortage "Growing Worse"', *The Times Educational Supplement*, **4328**, 31.

Dawson, Chester (1999), 'Japan's Jobs Dilemma', *Far Eastern Economic Review*, **162** (40), 92–3.

DeCloet, Derek (1999), 'Only the Good Go South', *Canadian Business*, **72** (13), 15–6.

Düll, Nicola (1998), *Changing Demographic Structures and Economic Performance in Germany*, Business Process Resource Center, Professional Development and Training Seminar Series, http://bprc.warwick.ac.uk/bprc31.htm, 14 July.

European Commission, (2000), Strategies for Jobs in the Information Society, http://www.europa,eu.int/comm./dg05/soc-dial/inf_soc/index_en.htm.

The European Social Fund, an Overview of the Programming Period 1994–99 (1998), European Social Fund Report, March.

Europemedia.net (2000), 'EU Skills Shortage "Stifling Start-Up Growth Rates"' http://www.europemedia.net/showfeature.asp?ArticleID=49, 16 May.

Ewing, Jack and H. Dawly (1999), 'The Missing Worker', *Business Week*, **3661,** 70–1.

Fiorino, Frances (2000), 'Wanted: Skilled Airline Mechanics', *Aviation Week & Space Technology*, **152** (16), 91–3.

Gingras, Yves and R. Roy (1998), *Is There a Skill Gap in Canada?*, Canadian Public Policy **26** (0) Supplement July, 5159–74.

Guth, Rob, C. Haney, D. Legard and T. Uimonen (1998), 'Despite Rampant Unemployment, Lack of IT Skills Threatens Asian Growth', *ComputerWorld*, **32** (49).

Hatch, Julie and A. Clinton (2000), 'Job Growth in the 1990s: A Retrospect', *Monthly Labor Review*, **123** (12), 3–18.

Heijke, Hans (ed.) (1994), *Forecasting the Labor Market By Occupation And Education: The Forecasting Activities of Three European Labour Market Research Institutes*, Dordrecht: Kluwer Academic.

'Hospitals May Help Relieve Nurse Shortage' (2000), *Health Care Strategic Management*, **19** (5).

Inagami, Takeshi (1998), *Labor Market Policies in Asian Countries*, International Labor Organization, Department of Employment and Training, Mèrneo working paper.

Infocomm Development Authority of Singapore (2000), 'S$2 Million Set Aside to Train Infocomm Specialists', http://ida.gov.sg/newsroom/mediarelease/2000/6Jul2000/, 6 July.

Jeong, Jooyeon (1996), 'Two Types of Labor Shortage: The Case of the Korean Machine Tool Industry', *Journal of Industry Studies*, **3** (1), 71–85.

Lynch, Lisa M. (2000), 'What Might Stall the Engine of the Economy', *Economic Outlook of 2001*, Department of Economics, Ann Arbor, MI: University of Michigan, 280–95.

'Manpower Shortage Slows Growth' (2000), *Industry Week*, **249** (8), 14.

Minnesota Department of Economic Security, Research and Planning Branch (2000), *Job Openings by Occupation in the Twin Cities*, Minneapolis, MN, August.

Pappone, Jeff (2000), 'Shrinking Skill Pool Threatens Living Standard: Severe Labor Shortages are on the Horizon', *Ottawa Citizen*, 6 May.

Richter, M. J. (2000), 'Job Shortages', *Telephony*, 27 March, 14–16.

Roberts, Alison (1999/2000) 'High-tech Portugal', *Europe*, **392**, 25–6.

Sherefkin, Robert (2000), 'Joint Venture Tackles Auto Industry Labour Shortage', *Automotive News*, **74** (5874), 10.

Skill Shortage in Australia's IT&T Industry (1998), Department of Communications, Information Technology and the Arts, the Department of Education, Training and Youth Affairs, the Department of Employment, Workplace Relations and Small Business and the Department of Immigration and Multicultural Affairs discussion paper.

'SMC and Partners Make Modest Progress in Addressing Microelectronics Skills Shortage' (2000), *Electronics Communicator*, **30** (28), 1–3.

US Department of Commerce (1999), Economic Trends and Outlooks: Belgium, National Trade Data Bank, http://www.tradeport.org/ts/countries/belgium/trends.html.

US Federal Reserve Board (2000), 'The Beige Book' http://www.federalreserve.gov/FOMC/BeigeBook/2000/20000503, 3 March.

Veneri, Carolyn M. (1999), 'Can Occupational Labor Shortages Be Identified Using Available Data?', *Monthly Labor Review*, **122** (3), 15–21.

Watson, Sharon (2001), 'Land of Plenty', *Computerworld*, **35** (11), 46.

5. Shortage indicators by occupation and country

This chapter has three purposes. Firstly, it discusses the methodology of measuring skill shortages, the data employed and the results. Secondly, the anecdotal information in Chapter 4 is related to the indicators in this chapter. Thirdly, the internal consistency of the indicators developed in this chapter is analysed.

Four indicators were used to measure labour shortages in the 19 countries studied. Not all four indicators were available in each country. The indicators were developed for up to 47 occupational groups. Not all groups could be obtained in each country. In some countries groups had to be further aggregated because the detail was not available. The four indicators used were: average annual employment growth by occupation 1995–98, unemployment rate average 1996–98 by occupation, average annual wage change by occupation 1995–98, and the amount of time required to prepare for the occupation. In two countries, Australia and Sweden, data for the exact period could not be obtained, so data from 1997–98 in Sweden and 1997–99 in Australia were used.

Ranks of 1 to 5 were assigned for each occupation in each country using the same criteria. A rank of 5 meant the labour market indicator was most favourable to the worker and most likely to indicate a labour shortage. For example, if employment grew an average of 4 per cent or more per year from 1995 to 1998 in an occupation in a country, a rank of 5 was assigned to this occupational group in that country. If employment declined, a rank of 1 was assigned. The unweighted average of the indicators in each occupation was then taken. An average rank close to 5 would be more likely to indicate a skill shortage and an average near 1 would be more likely to indicate a surplus of workers. In measuring employment changes or unemployment rates, data from government household surveys were favoured. The theoretical justification for the indicators measuring labour shortages was discussed in Chapter 2. No single indicator is sufficient to measure shortages, but taken together they offer a compelling explanation of what is happening in the labour market.

The obvious advantage of our ranking system is that it can be applied consistently over time and the number of occupations that we classified as possible shortages will rise and fall as conditions change in each country. At any point in time countries are in different stages of the business cycle but indicators used for each occupation will reflect these differences.

In previous work, Cohen (1995) used seven indicators to measure labour shortages in the United States. The other three indicators used in his work included replacement demand for labour, occupational employment forecasts and immigrants admitted in jobs for which United States workers could not be found.[1] Replacement demand is a measure of how many workers are hired to replace workers that leave the occupation. These indicators could not be replicated in other countries. By comparing the number of admitted workers to the size of the labour force in each occupation the immigration indicator was developed for the United States. More recently Cohen and Zaidi (1998) developed shortage indicators for the three North American Free Trade Agreement (NAFTA) countries, and also presented preliminary results for five countries (Cohen and Zaidi, 2000).

Few countries collect data on vacancies. The United Kingdom collects data on job vacancies by occupation and the United States is planning to collect this type of data in the future. Some local United States state government agencies such as the Minnesota Department of Economic Security (2000) collect job vacancy data. While job vacancy data can be a useful measure of shortages of workers, they alone are not enough to determine if a shortage exists. A more complete analysis of labour market conditions would be required to understand the dynamics of the market for a particular occupation. For example, job vacancies can exist in an occupation with high turnover and a high unemployment rate. The analysis of vacancy rates and unemployment rates in an occupation tells a lot more about labour shortages than only one indicator. Therefore the unemployment rate has been used as a proxy for excess labour demand and the importance of the relationship between unfilled vacancies and unemployment has been recognized. Efforts have been made to examine the condition of excess demand in the labour market in terms of vacancy and unemployment data (Zaidi, 1970; Siebert and Zaidi, 1994). The objective of these efforts has been to relate the statistics of unemployment and of unfilled vacancies, and design indices of the pressure of labour demand. The results show that the data on unfilled vacancies can be related successfully to unemployment figures and meaningful indices can be constructed on the basis of the relationship between those two measures. These indices can be used to reflect the low and high periods of excess labour demand.

COUNTRIES SELECTED

Nineteen counties were selected for study. The methodology relied on sample survey data from government sources or international organizations such as the International Labour Organization (ILO) and Eurostat. The selection was limited to countries large enough to have sufficient numbers of workers in the various occupations being studied. Similarly, only countries where labour statistics were available were studied. Finally, the analysis was limited to countries with consistent series. Skill shortages probably exist in small underdeveloped countries as well. However, the methodology used here cannot address this problem. Countries from North America, Latin America, Europe and the Pacific region were studied to obtain geographic diversity. The countries studied were the United States, Canada, Chile, Mexico, Austria, Belgium, Denmark, France, Germany, Greece, Italy, Portugal, Spain, Sweden, the United Kingdom, Australia, Japan, Singapore and the Republic of Korea.

OCCUPATIONAL DEFINITIONS

In order to compare occupational shortages around the world it is necessary to have standardized occupational definitions. The International Standard Classification of Occupations (ISCO-88) was chosen as the system to be used to compare occupational indicators in the 19 countries. The 14th International Conference of Labour Statisticians developed the standard and it is based in part on the average skill level of the workers in each occupation (Elias, 1997). Unfortunately several of the countries, including the United States, do not use ISCO-88 as their standard occupational classification system.

ISCO-88 has ten major groups. Within the major groups are sub-groups of occupations. The major groups are based on educational qualifications. For example, professionals require a university degree. Technicians and associate professionals require training beyond secondary education. Clerks, service workers, skilled agricultural workers, craft workers and plant and machine operators require secondary education. Elementary occupations require only five years or a grade school education. Legislators and armed forces are not classified by skill level.

Australia uses the Australian Standard Classification of Occupations (ASCO) classification system, which required conversion to ISCO-88.[2] Canada and the United Kingdom use their own Standard Occupational Classification Systems.[3] The United States has a Census of Population occupational system, which differs markedly from ISCO-88 (US Department of Commerce, Bureau of Census, 1992). The United States system is being replaced by a new Standard Occupational Classification system that will be more skill-based (US Department of Labor, Bureau of Labor Statistics, 1999). The first data on the new United States classification system were published in 2001 for the Occupational Employment Survey; however, only establishment data for 1999 were published. In order to make cross-country comparisons United States codes had to be converted to ISCO-88 codes. This was not easy because the United States Census classification system is not skill-based. ISCO-88 separates professionals and associate professionals while the United States in many cases combines them in the same occupation. Unpublished data from many of the European countries were made available by Eurostat using ISCO-88 codes. Data for some countries are only available for major occupational groups. These data are collected by the International Labour Office (ILO, 2001).

The occupational groups in this book were developed to provide as much occupational detail as possible. However, because the estimates are based on samples in the various countries and the standard errors from the samples were not always available, an occupational cell size of 25 000 for employment was selected as a desirable minimum size for cross-country comparison. When this size was not achieved the cell was typically not used in the tables. Eurostat offers cell size guidelines for publication of their data. These guidelines vary by country but are in the range of 4500–8500. Data below these thresholds are sometimes published with a warning. The technique employed here involved computing percentage change and making cross-country and cross-occupation comparison, and required a larger minimum cell size.

ISCO-88 occupational groups are defined at the one-, two-, three- and four-digit levels. Four-digit groups offer the most occupational detail. Greater detail was used for professional, associate professional and technical occupations where more training and preparation is required. This analysis was based on groupings of ISCO-88 two- and three-digit occupations. Forty-seven groups were defined based on this minimum size. Table 5.1 shows the groups used.

Table 5.1 Summary of occupation groups

Group	Title	ISCO Codes
1A	Government officials, CEOs, senior managers[a]	111–4, 121–3, 131
1B	Production & operations department managers	122
2A	Physicists, chemists & related professionals	211
2B	Mathematicians, statisticians & related prof.	212
2C	Computing professionals	213
2D	Architects, engineers & related professionals	214
2E	Life science professionals	221
2F	Health professionals (except nursing)	222
2G	Nursing & midwifery professionals	223
2H	College, univ. & higher educ. teaching prof.	231
2I	Secondary education teaching professionals	232
2J	Primary & pre-primary education professionals	233
2K	Special education teaching professionals	234
2L	Other teaching professionals	235
2M	Business professionals	241
2N	Legal professionals	242
2O	Archivists, librarians & related info. prof.	243
2P	Social sciences & related professionals	244
2Q	Writers & creative or performing artists	245
2R	Religious professionals	246
3A	Physical & engineering science technicians	311
3B	Computer associate professionals	312
3C	Optical & electronic equipment operators	313
3D	Ship & aircraft controllers & technicians	314
3E	Safety & quality inspectors	315
3F	Life science technicians & related assoc. prof.	321
3G	Modern & traditional health associate professionals (except nursing)	322, 324

Table 5.1 Summary of occupation groups (continued)

Group	Title	ISCO Codes
3H	Nursing & midwifery associate professionals	323
3I	Teaching associate professionals	331–4
3J	Business & administrative associate prof.	341–3
3K	Police & government inspectors & detectives[b]	344–5
3L	Religious, artistic & social work assoc. prof.	346–8
4	Clerks	411–22
5A	Travel attendants & related workers	511
5B	Housekeeping & restaurant service workers	512
5C	Personal care & related workers	513
5D	Other personal service workers	514–5
5E	Protective services workers	516
5F	Models, salespersons & demonstrators	521–3
6	Skilled agriculture and fishery workers	611–21
7A	Extraction and building trade workers	711–4
7B	Precision and related trades workers[c]	721–4, 731, 742–4
7C	Handicraft workers of glass, metal, wood, & textiles[d]	732–4
7D	Food processing and related trades workers	741
8A	Stationary plant & machine operators & assemblers	811–7 821–9
8B	Drivers & mobile plant operators	831–4
9A	Elementary occupations[e]	911–33

Notes: [a] Includes other departmental managers and general managers

[b] Includes customs, tax and related government associate professionals

[c] Includes metal, machinery and related trades workers and other craft and related trades workers

[d] Includes potters, glass-makers, printers and related trades workers

[e] Includes sales and service elementary occupations, agricultural, fishery and related labourers, and labourers in mining, construction, manufacturing and transport

THE INDICATORS, THEIR MEASUREMENT AND THEIR LIMITATIONS

Employment Change

Employment change in an occupation reflects the increase in demand for workers in that occupation. Employment change by occupation was measured in each country from 1995 to 1998. Table 5.2 shows how the indicator was derived based upon employment change in each country.

Table 5.2 Employment growth indicator

Indicator Score	Average Annual Growth
5	4.0% or more
4	2.7 to 3.9%
3	1.4 to 2.6%
2	0.0 to 1.3%
1	Less than 0.0%

If the supply of labour was totally inelastic, shifts in the demand for labour would not increase employment. In such a case all that would happen is that wages would increase as employers bid against each other in order to obtain labour. Even if the supply of labour were highly inelastic, increases in demand for labour would come at a high price in terms of increasing wages.

The scenario of totally or even highly inelastic labour supply is not a common one. However, by using both the unemployment rate and wage change as indicators a better picture of labour market conditions can be captured than by indicator alone. Unfortunately wage change data were not available in most countries.

Another problem with using employment data as an indicator collected from household surveys is the possibility that the respondent may have mischaracterized their occupation. In the United States half of the sample responses to the Current Population Survey are based on proxy reporters, that is, another member of the household reports them. This can introduce errors (US Department of Commerce, 2000). Similarly, since employment data are based on a sample, sampling errors are introduced. These errors are most serious when the sample size is small. As employment is divided into many different occupations, sampling errors grow. Large enough occupational groups were chosen carefully in order to minimize sampling errors.

Unemployment Rate

The average unemployment rate was computed for 1996–98 by occupation in each country. Table 5.3 shows the scores assigned to different ranges of unemployment.

Table 5.3 Unemployment rate indicator

Indicator Score	Average Annual Unemployment Rate
5	0.0 to 1.9%
4	2.0 to 4.0%
3	4.1 to 6.0%
2	6.0 to 8.0%
1	More than 8.0%

Since the unemployment rate in most countries is based on a sample survey, the problems of classification and sample size discussed for employment change are true for the unemployment rate as well. In addition there are other problems with the use of the unemployment rate. Firstly, if the unemployment rate measures the last occupation of a person it may mischaracterize a person's skills. For example, if a university lecturer cannot find a job teaching and decides to drive a bus and then loses his job as a bus driver, the person might be characterized as an unemployed bus driver rather than an unemployed lecturer.

Secondly, there are differences in frictional unemployment levels among various occupations. For example, if it takes university lecturers longer to find jobs than it takes labourers even though there is no excess demand for either occupation, but the job search is more complex for professionals, the unemployment rate would be higher for university lecturers. However, if comparing excess demand by occupation a higher level of frictional unemployment would send a false signal.

Thirdly, it is nearly impossible to standardize for differences in occupational unemployment rates in different countries. The US Department of Labor, Bureau of Labor Statistics, OECD and Eurostat have produced standardized unemployment rates in ten countries (US Department of Labor, Bureau of Labor Statistics, 2000b). However, the standardization is for the overall unemployment rate. In order to properly standardize by occupation, one would have to have the actual sample of data in each country and determine how the differences affect each occupation. For example, if one country measures unemployment for persons 14 and over and another country measures unemployment for persons 16 and over, the unemployment rate may require significant adjustment for occupations employing youth, such as a retail stock person, but would require no adjustment for physicians. Since the differences are multidimensional the problems of adjustment are exponential. However, it is believed that the unadjusted values are worth including rather than omitting this important indicator.

Fourthly, there could be differences in a country's policy toward tolerance of unemployment or litigation costs, which could make it difficult for employers in some countries to lay off or dismiss workers. Thus the unemployment rate in an occupation could be low even with excess supply of workers because employers cannot readily dismiss these workers.

Wage Change

The change in wages from 1995 to 1998 was computed in countries where such information was available. The availability of this measure was more limited than the other indicators. Table 5.4 illustrates the cut-offs used.

Table 5.4 Wage growth indicator

	Average Annual Nominal Growth of Wages in Countries Where Prices Increased by	
Indicator Score	**More than 2.0%**	**Less than 2.0%**
5	5.0% or more	4.0% or more
4	3.3 to 4.9%	2.7 to 3.9%
3	1.6 to 3.2%	1.4 to 2.6%
2	0.0 to 1.5%	0.0 to 1.3%
1	Negative	Negative

The wage change measure can share some of the same problems as the previous two indicators. In addition, two other problems are present. Firstly, wages respond both to excess demand for labour and price level. A 5 per cent wage increase in a country with a 6 per cent rate of inflation is a lower real increase than a 3 per cent wage increase in a country with a 2 per cent rate of inflation. If wages and prices could be measured without error and the price index reflected real purchasing power of the worker, a strong argument could be made for using real rather than nominal wages. Because of errors in measurement and lags in prices and wages our wage indicator allows for two different levels of inflation and is otherwise based on nominal wage increases. Secondly, wages could be unresponsive to increases in demand for labour due to government constraints on changing wages or trade union contracts. Finally, since we had wage data for only five countries with minimal differences in inflation, the use of two different indicator tables was adequate to account for differences in inflation in the five countries.

As with all the other indicators it is believed that while the indicator alone is not ideal, when combined with other indicators it can give a reliable picture of potential shortages.

Occupational Training Time

Finally, an indicator was developed that measures occupational training time required in an occupation. Because the indicator is broad, differences in training time across countries were not thought to be significant. For example, medical school may require six years in one country and five in another but in both instances training beyond a bachelor's degree is required. Therefore occupations were assigned the same score in a given occupational group across countries. Table 5.5 shows how the scores were determined.

Table 5.5 Training indicator

Indicator Score	Level of Training
5	More than a Bachelor's Degree
4	Bachelor's Degree
3	Associate's Degree
2	Vocational or Long-Term On-the-Job Training
1	Moderate- or Short-Term On-the-Job Training

One could argue that this measure is not truly an indicator of shortages and may artificially increase the likelihood of skilled occupations being considered shortage occupations. In a country with an oversupply of college-trained workers, occupations requiring a college degree would be more likely to be considered a shortage occupation simply because it requires more training when compared to another occupation requiring only a high school degree. This is an obvious problem with the training indicator. If a shortage develops in an occupation with a long training time, then that shortage will be harder to alleviate than in an occupation where the training time is short because many more workers are available to perform work requiring less skill. Workers can perform the less-skilled work as a secondary job, when retired from another job or while in school. However, some jobs, like toxic waste collector, may be so unpleasant that even though they may not require a lot of training they may be hard to fill. This again illustrates why one indicator alone may not predict whether or not there is a shortage in any one occupation, but when combined with other indicators can be a good predictor.

The Appendix presents the results of the indicators in each of the 19 countries for as many of the 47 occupational groups for which reliable data could be obtained. Table 5.6 summarizes the results obtained by country for the nine major occupational groups. These nine groups are aggregates of the 47 detailed occupational groups. A score of 3.75 to 5.0 for an occupational group would be most likely to have shortages. A score of 1.0 to 2.25 would be most likely to have labour surpluses. Groups with indicator averages between 2.25 and 3.75 are not as likely to have shortages or surpluses.

Of the 19 countries, ten had scores from 3.75 to 5.0 for legislators, senior officials and managers and nine for professionals. Japan data could not be computed for senior officials and managers. No country had an average score from 1.0 to 2.25 for professionals or senior officials and managers. However, since training required for professionals had a score of four, a score below 2.25 was very unlikely when other indicators were averaged. Australia, Italy and Mexico had the highest scores of 4.67 for legislators, senior officials and managers. France and Germany had the lowest scores of 2.5 to 2.67. No country was in the range where surpluses were likely. Since these are averages this does not preclude a shortage or surplus in a specialized occupation in any country. Austria, Greece, the Republic of Korea, Mexico and Singapore had the highest indicator scores of 4.67 for professionals while France, Denmark, Japan and Sweden had the lowest scores of 2.67 to 3.0. Only three countries were in the range for shortages for technicians and associate professionals: Republic of Korea, Singapore and Mexico. No shortages were exhibited in any other country in any of the other six occupational groups except craft workers in Mexico.

Some occupational groups in some countries actually had average scores of 1.0: France for clerks; Belgium, Germany and Japan for plant and machine operators and assemblers; and Belgium, Germany, Greece, Italy, Japan and the United Kingdom for elementary occupations such as helpers, labourers, cleaners and handlers.

Table 5.6 Indicator averages for major occupational groups

	Occupational Group								
Country (no. of indicators)	**1**	**2**	**3**	**4**	**5**	**6**	**7**	**8**	**9**
Australia (3)	4.67	4.33	3.33	2.67	2.33	2.00	2.00	2.33	2.00
Austria (3)	4.00	4.67	3.33	2.00	2.67	3.00	2.00	1.67	1.33
Belgium (3)	3.33	3.67	2.67	1.67	1.67	2.33	1.33	1.00	1.00
Canada (4)	3.00	3.25	3.25	2.25	2.00	1.50	2.25	2.50	2.00
Chile (3)	4.33	4.33	3.00	2.67	2.67	2.67	–	–	–
Denmark (3)	4.33	3.00	3.67	1.33	2.00	2.33	2.33	1.33	2.33
France (2)	2.50	2.67	2.33	1.00	2.00	1.50	1.50	1.67	1.67
Germany (3)	2.67	3.67	3.00	1.33	1.33	1.33	1.33	1.00	1.00
Greece (3)	4.33	4.67	3.67	1.33	1.67	2.67	1.67	2.67	1.00
Italy (3)	4.67	4.33	3.00	2.00	1.67	2.33	1.67	1.67	1.00
Japan (3)	–	3.00	2.33	1.33	1.67	1.33	1.67	1.00	1.00
Republic of Korea (3)	3.00	4.67	4.00	2.00	2.67	2.67	2.00	2.00	2.00
Mexico (3)	4.67	4.67	4.33	3.33	3.33	2.67	4.00	3.33	3.33
Portugal (3)	3.33	3.33	3.00	2.00	2.33	2.67	3.67	3.33	3.33
Singapore (3)	4.33	4.67	4.33	3.33	3.33	–	–	–	–

Table 5.6 Indicator averages for major occupational groups (continued)

	Occupational Group								
Country (no. of indicators)	**1**	**2**	**3**	**4**	**5**	**6**	**7**	**8**	**9**
Spain (3)	3.67	3.67	3.00	1.33	1.67	2.00	2.00	1.33	1.67
Sweden (3)	4.00	3.00	3.33	2.00	3.00	2.00	2.67	2.33	1.33
United Kingdom (3)	3.33	3.67	3.33	2.00	2.00	1.67	2.00	1.67	1.00
United States (4)	4.00	3.75	3.25	2.25	2.00	2.00	2.75	2.00	2.00

Notes: Occupational group codes definitions:

Major Group 1: Legislators, senior officials and managers
Major Group 2: Professionals
Major Group 3: Technicians and associate professionals
Major Group 4: Clerks
Major Group 5: Service workers and shop and market sales workers
Major Group 6: Skilled agricultural and fishery workers
Major Group 7: Craft and related trades workers
Major Group 8: Plant and machine operators and assemblers
Major Group 9: Elementary occupations

Source: Calculated from compiled data. See Appendix.

Table 5.7 illustrates the detailed occupational groups with the highest indicator scores by country. Detailed occupational data were not available for Chile, Republic of Korea, Mexico and Singapore. Italy had scores of 3.75 or more in every one of the occupations. The United States had scores in this range for all occupations except social sciences and related professionals and computer associate professionals. Greece had occupations in the shortage range in all of the occupations in the table.

Certain occupations, such as computing professionals and CEOs, had skill shortage candidates in most countries. Of course, within a country, shortages can exist in any occupation even if the overall unemployment rate is low enough. For example, in the United States in Ann Arbor, Michigan, where the unemployment rate had been hovering around 2 per cent, there have been shortages of retail clerks, clerical employees and certain construction workers.

Table 5.8 highlights occupations with the lowest scores in the study. Personal care and related workers scored under 2.25 in only two countries and was the strongest of the low indicator score occupations. It would probably not be classified as an occupation with surplus workers except in Denmark and Greece. Stationary plant and machine operators and assemblers are in the surplus range in all countries except Canada, Greece and Portugal.

ANECDOTAL VALIDATION

Table 5.9 compares the external information discussed in Chapter 4 with the shortage indicators developed in this chapter. For the most part the internal information is consistent with the indicator scores reported previously.

Several reasons for possible inconsistencies exist. The anecdotal reporting is not based on a consistent (let alone rigorous) methodology, the time periods may differ and the occupational definitions may differ. For example, in the United States all occupations identified anecdotally as shortages, except health professionals and nursing and midwifery professionals, were in the shortage range using the indicators developed in this chapter. These two occupations had been among those Cohen (1995) identified as having very high scores in 1995. This may be simply a timing discrepancy between our current study and the anecdotal reporting.

The US Department of Labor, Bureau of Labor Statistics (1999) published a study of labour shortages in 1998. The study yields results

Table 5.7 Occupations with high indicator scores

	Occupation									
Country	1A	2C	2D	2F	2H	2M	2N	2P	3B	3G
Australia	–	4.33	3.33	3.00	3.67	4.67	3.67	–	–	4.33
Austria	4.67	–	–	3.67	–	4.33	–	–	3.67	3.67
Belgium	3.67	4.67	3.33	4.67	–	4.33	4.67	4.33	-	2.67
Canada	3.50	–	–	–	–	3.50	–	–	–	–
Denmark	4.67	–	2.67	3.33	–	3.00	–	–	–	4.00
France	3.00	3.33	3.00	3.50	3.00	–	3.00	3.00	2.00	2.50
Germany	3.00	4.33	3.67	–	3.33	4.33	4.67	4.00	3.00	4.00
Greece	4.33	–	4.67	4.67	–	4.00	5.00	–	–	–
Italy	5.00	–	4.67	5.00	5.00	4.67	5.00	–	4.00	4.00
Japan	–	4.00	–	2.33	3.50	–	–	–	3.00	4.00
Portugal	–	–	3.33	–	–	–	–	–	2.67	–
Spain	4.00	4.00	4.33	4.33	5.00	3.33	4.67	3.33	3.00	3.00
Sweden	4.67	3.33	3.00	4.00	3.67	4.00	–	4.00	–	3.00
United Kingdom	3.33	4.33	3.67	4.00	3.67	4.33	5.00	3.33	3.00	4.33
United States	4.50	4.25	3.75	3.75	4.00	3.75	3.75	3.50	3.00	3.75

Notes: Occupational sub-group codes definitions:

Code	Definition
1A	Government officials, CEOs, senior managers
2C	Computing professionals
2D	Architects, engineers and related professionals
2F	Health professionals (except nursing)
2H	College, university and higher education teaching professionals
2M	Business professionals
2N	Legal professionals
2P	Social sciences and related professionals
3B	Computer associate professionals
3G	Modern and traditional health associate professionals (except nursing)

Source: Calculated from compiled data. See Appendix.

Table 5.8 Occupations with low indicator scores

	Occupation			
Country	**5C**	**5F**	**8A**	**8B**
Australia	3.00	–	1.67	3.00
Austria	2.33	3.00	1.67	1.67
Belgium	2.33	1.33	1.33	1.33
Canada	–	2.25	2.75	2.00
Denmark	2.00	2.00	1.00	2.00
France	3.00	1.67	1.50	2.00
Germany	2.67	1.00	1.00	1.00
Greece	1.00	2.00	2.33	2.33
Italy	2.33	1.67	1.67	1.67
Japan	–	2.67	1.00	1.00
Portugal	3.67	3.33	3.33	3.67
Spain	2.33	2.33	1.33	1.33
Sweden	2.67	2.33	1.00	1.00
United Kingdom	3.00	2.00	1.33	1.67
United States	2.75	2.00	1.75	2.25

Notes: Occupational sub-group codes definitions:

- 5C Personal care and related workers
- 5F Models, salespersons and demonstrators
- 8A Stationary plant and machine operators and assemblers
- 8B Drivers and mobile plant operators

Source: Calculated from compiled data. See Appendix.

Table 5.9 Indicator scores of detailed skilled occupations mentioned as shortage occupations in Chapter 4

Country	Occupation	Indicator Score
Australia	Computing professionals	4.33
	Nurses	3.67
Germany	Software engineers	4.33
Singapore	Professionals	4.67
United States	Management analysts	3.75
	Special education teachers	4.50
	Nurses	3.25
	Computer scientists	4.25
	Physicians	3.25
United Kingdom	Computer scientists	4.33

similar to those in this book; however, that study relies heavily on Cohen (1995) and is not an independent test. The study also cites anecdotal information about shortages of construction workers, which would not be rated as a shortage based on the indicators presented here but was found to be a shortage in the United States using anecdotal information.

Our indicators may understate the shortage for construction workers to the extent that construction is a seasonal occupation. The average annual unemployment rate may be high but in the prime months for construction activity, such as spring and summer, the unemployment rate could be low – consistent with the shortage theory.

Another problem with the craft and related trades workers category is that it gets a lower indicator score for training. If we could separate out apprenticable trades that require long training periods then that segment of the occupation would get a much higher indicator score.

MEASURES OF INTERNAL CONSISTENCY

The previous sections of the chapter discussed how the shortage indicators were explained by various economy-wide measures in the 19 countries in this study. Another series of tests that can be applied pertain to internal consistency of the measures.

In the ideal world we would be able to validate our model by comparing our estimates of shortages to the actual measure of shortages. However, there is no actual measure of shortages. The significance of the relationship between the components that make up the shortage ranks can be measured using an F-test from an analysis of variance. It is possible to contrast this probability between countries to determine if the data from any of the countries is much less reliable than the data from any other country. However, the prime interest here is in the Cronbach's Alpha.

Cronbach's Alpha measures the correlation between various components of a single measure. If the correlation among the measures is high this suggests they are measuring the same phenomenon. It should be noted that the use here of these measures differs from their normal use. The normal use is, for example, to test if several raters are providing consistent ratings on employees, such as in performance reviews. If the ratings differ substantially there may be problems with the system being used. If the correlation is low this suggests they may not be reliable. A recent use of Cronbach's Alpha can be found in Kleiner and Ham (2001). In this study they explored the intercorrelation of various industrial relations variables.

There are theoretical reasons for some of the measures used in this book to yield different predictions for the same occupation. For example, if labour supply is totally inelastic, wages in an occupation could be rapidly increasing while employment growth would be zero. In this example employment growth is uncorrelated with labour shortages. Similarly, in a country with institutional barriers, which prevent wages from reacting quickly, wage growth might be slow even when employment is growing rapidly. It is believed that combining the indicators gives the best measure. However, it is expected that over a three-year period there are very few instances of totally inelastic supply because countries can use training and immigration to increase supply.

In this application, different ranking systems could produce different results due to differing economic conditions in the various countries (as in the previous example of an inelastic supply of labour). It is interesting to see the countries in which the measures are least consistent. Tables 5.10 and 5.11 show this correlation. Table 5.10 shows the correlation for the nine summary occupations, and is summarized by Cronbach's Alpha. This measure does not work well when correlations are negative. In several countries – Australia, Austria, Germany, Italy, the United Kingdom and the United States – Cronbach's Alpha is 0.8 or higher. These are all countries with reasonably good labour statistics systems. They are also larger countries where samples would be large enough so that standard errors are small for the individual indicators. It should be noted that in two of the countries four indicators are used and in four of the countries only three of the indicators were available, yet Cronbach's Alpha was high, suggesting internal consistency in both cases.

Table 5.10 Correlation coefficients and Cronbach's Alpha – summary occupations

	Training		Unemp Rate	Wage Change					
Country	**Emp Growth**	**Unemp Rate**	**Emp Growth**	**Train-ing**	**Emp Growth**	**Unemp Rate**	**Cronbach's Alpha**	**Number of Cases**	**Prob***
Australia	0.550	0.645	0.508	–	–	–	0.796	9	0.012
Austria	0.635	0.741	0.508	–	–	–	0.823	9	0.001
Belgium	0.493	0.730	0.237	–	–	–	0.743	9	0.191
Chile	0.369	0.484	-0.097	–	–	–	0.535	6	0.094
Denmark	0.193	0.804	-0.169	–	–	–	0.439	9	0.365
Germany	0.558	0.833	0.614	–	–	–	0.850	9	0.358
Greece	0.524	0.822	0.307	–	–	–	0.747	9	0.290
Italy	0.854	0.743	0.648	–	–	–	0.895	9	0.002
Republic of Korea	0.496	0.310	0.341	–	–	–	0.603	9	0.001
Mexico	0.033	0.831	-0.316	–	–	–	0.263	9	0.000
Portugal	-0.529	0.851	-0.705	–	–	–	-1.591	9	0.011
Singapore	-0.516	0.963	-0.408	–	–	–	0.300	9	0.000
Spain	0.714	0.608	-0.058	–	–	–	0.698	9	0.007
United Kingdom	0.364	0.822	0.620	–	–	–	0.816	9	0.171
Canada	-0.291	0.743	-0.196	-0.263	-0.174	0.035	0.118	9	–
United States	0.820	0.831	0.802	0.174	0.249	-0.144	0.822	9	0.017
France	-0.556	–	–	0.556	-1.000	–	-0.333	4	0.729
Japan	0.789	–	–	0.356	0.539	–	0.763	8	0.445
Sweden	0.088	–	–	0.394	0.112	–	0.420	8	0.004

Note: *Probability based on an F-test from an analysis of variance.

Table 5.11 Correlation coefficients and Cronbach's Alpha – detailed occupations

	Training		Unemp Rate	Wage Change					
Country	**Emp Growth**	**Unemp Rate**	**Emp Growth**	**Train-ing**	**Emp Growth**	**Unemp Rate**	**Cronbach's Alpha**	**Number of Cases**	**Prob***
Australia	-0.121	0.675	0.044	–	–	–	0.310	27	0.006
Austria	0.146	0.208	-0.122	–	–	–	0.164	26	0.003
Belgium	0.233	0.638	-0.022	–	–	–	0.530	26	0.594
Chile	–	–	–	–	–	–	–	–	–
Denmark	-0.137	0.390	-0.017	–	–	–	0.097	21	0.047
Germany	0.225	0.404	0.245	–	–	–	0.535	41	0.765
Greece	0.278	0.721	0.380	–	–	–	0.715	23	0.034
Italy	0.444	0.565	0.358	–	–	–	0.695	32	0.001
Republic of Korea	–	–	–	–	–	–	–	–	–
Mexico	–	–	–	–	–	–	–	–	–
Portugal	-0.542	0.330	-0.289	–	–	–	-1.238	16	0.000
Singapore	–	–	–	–	–	–	–	–	–
Spain	0.484	0.601	0.287	–	–	–	0.715	33	0.000
United Kingdom	-0.011	0.634	0.124	–	–	–	0.439	42	0.140
Canada	0.119	0.721	-0.142	-0.056	-0.254	0.190	0.374	11	0.389
France	0.783	–	–	-0.354	-0.227	–	0.384	7	0.792
Japan	0.092	–	–	0.353	-0.127	–	0.203	22	0.615
Sweden	0.002	–	–	0.152	-0.327	–	-0.258	22	0.011
United States	0.267	0.706	0.066	0.040	-0.166	0.098	0.489	42	0.000

Note: *Probability based on an F-test from an analysis of variance

Table 5.11 reflects the correlations for the more detailed occupations. Because the sample sizes are smaller and the methodology and sources used to develop the variables are more diverse, much lower correlations are observed. In fact not a single country has a Cronbach's Alpha of 0.8 or higher. If the measures were raters rating the same individuals, these low scores would be of greater concern than in their present use; however, the statistics are provided as a further way of analysing the indicators.

France had only four summary occupations for which we had observations on employment growth and wage growth (see Table 5.12). The three occupations that required some amount of skill had identical indicators for employment growth and wage growth. Only elementary occupations had a disparity. However, the disparity was enough to result in a perfectly negative correlation for the four occupations (see Figure 5.1).

Table 5.12 Summary occupations – with observations on employment growth and wage growth

Occupation	Employment Growth	Wage Growth
Professionals	2	2
Technicians	2	2
Machine operators	2	2
Elementary occupations	3	1

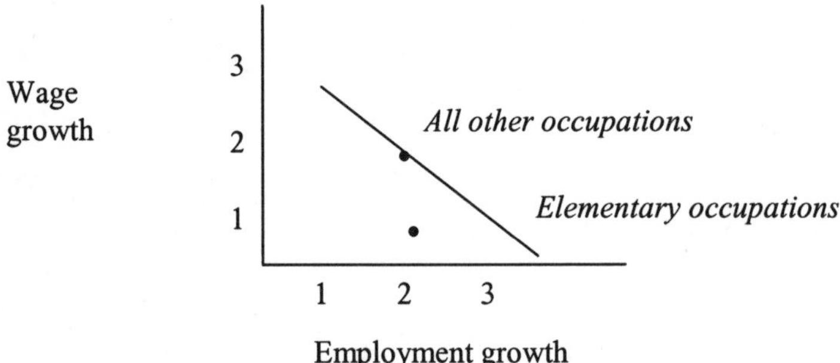

Figure 5.1 Relationship between indicators – France

SUMMARY

A set of consistent indicators to measure shortages was developed for up to 49 occupations in 19 countries. These indicators were based on the unemployment rate, growth in employment, growth in wages and amount of training required in the occupation. To test the reliability of the indicators they were compared to anecdotal information collected in Chapter 4 and found to be reasonably consistent.

Internal consistency was tested using Cronbach's Alpha. For the major occupation groups the consistency was good in countries with reliable data. For detailed occupational groups where the data were based on different data collected from many different countries, the consistency was not as good. Cronbach's Alpha was also used to test the internal validity of the measures. The measures were fairly consistent in larger countries when summary groups were examined but varied considerably when detailed occupations or smaller countries were considered.

Notes:

1. The US Department of Labor, Bureau of Labor Statistics (2000a) makes occupational forecasts for the United States every two years. Under current US immigration law immigrants can be admitted if there is a labour market need. Unpublished data on the admitted workers by occupation was obtained by Cohen (1995).
2. We thank the Australian Bureau of Statistics for assistance, to Eurostat for their conversions of several countries and to ILO for conversions of major groups.
3. We are indebted to Wayne Silver and Marc Levesque of Statistics Canada. Mr. Silver assisted us in converting the Canadian system to ISCO-88 and Mr. Levesque helped us obtain special tabulations of Canadian data. Statistics Canada information is used with the permission of the Minister of Industry, as Minister responsible for Statistics Canada. Information on the availability of the wide range of data from Statistics Canada can be obtained from Statistics Canada's Regional Offices, its World Wide Web site at http:/www.statcan.ca, and its toll-free access number 1-800-263-1136.

REFERENCES

Cohen, Malcolm S. (1995), *Labor Shortages as America Approaches the Twenty-first Century*, Ann Arbor, MI: University of Michigan Press.

Cohen, Malcolm S. and M. Zaidi (1998), 'Labor Shortages, Pay and Training in NAFTA Countries', *North American Journal of Economics and Finance*, **9** (1), 89–103.

Cohen, Malcolm S. and M. Zaidi (2000), 'Global Skill Shortages', *Proceedings of the 48th Annual Conference On The Economic and Social Outlook*, Ann Arbor, MI: University of Michigan.

Elias, Peter (1997), 'Occupational Classification (ISCO-88): Concepts, Methods, Reliability, Validity and Cross-National Comparability', *Occasional Papers No. 20*, Organization for Economic Cooperation and Development, Labor Market and Social Policy, Paris.

Yearbook of Labour Statistics (2000), 59th Issue, Geneva: International Labour Office, Copyright © International Labour Organization 2001.

Kleiner, Morris M. and H. Ham (2001), 'Do Industrial Relations Institutions Affect Economic Efficiency?: International and U.S. State-Level Evidence', Paper to be presented at the Industrial Relations Center, 12 October, Minneapolis, MN.

Minnesota Department of Economic Security (2000), *Job Openings by Occupation in the Twin Cities*, Minneapolis, MN.

Siebert, Calvin D. and M. Zaidi (1994), 'Measuring Excess Demand and Unemployment in Canada and the United States', *Relations Industrielles*, **49** (3), 503–26.

US Department of Commerce, Bureau of Census (1992), 'Classified Index of Industries and Occupations', Washington, DC.

US Department of Commerce, Economics and Statistics Administration, US Department of Commerce, Bureau of Census and US Department of Labor, Bureau of Labor Statistics (2000), 'Current Population Survey, Design and Methodology', *Technical Paper 63*, Washington, DC.

US Department of Labor, Bureau of Labor Statistics (1999), 'Revising the Standard Occupational Classification System', *Report 929*, Washington, DC.

US Department of Labor, Bureau of Labor Statistics (2000a), *Occupational Projections and Training Data*, Washington, DC.

US Department of Labor, Bureau of Labor Statistics (2000b), *Comparative Civilian Labor Force Statistics Ten Countries 1959–99*, Washington, DC.

Zaidi, Mahmood A. (1970), 'Unemployment, Vacancies and Conditions of Excess Demand for Labor in Canada', *Applied Economics*, **2** (2), 101–12.

6. Factors correlated with shortages

This chapter examines the factors that could explain shortages and labour surpluses. The relationship between the shortage indicators and other indicators in the 19 countries is analysed. While the emphasis is on the nine major occupational group indicators, some analysis is done for detailed occupations such as college and university professionals.

FACTORS AFFECTING SHORTAGES

In order to systematically measure differences across countries in institutions, policies, demographics and economic conditions, variables compiled by the Economist Intelligence Unit (EIU) (2001) were used. They compiled hundreds of indicators for many countries including the 19 included in this study. The variables fall into six general categories:

1. Macroeconomic indicators
2. Demographics and health
3. Consumer markets and income
4. Infrastructure
5. Competitiveness
6. Politics, institutions and regulations.

Within each of these broad groups there are sub-groups and within each sub-group there are individual indicators. For example, within the group 'politics, institutions and regulations' there are seven sub-groups:

1. EIU business environment ratings
2. Private enterprise
3. Labour market
4. Tax regime
5. Financing
6. Foreign trade and exchange
7. Policy toward foreign investment.

Within the sub-group 'labour market' there are five measures:

1. Industrial relations
2. Restrictiveness of labour laws
3. Wage regulation
4. Hiring of foreign nationals
5. Working days lost to strikes.

Since the emphasis of this book is on the labour market, more attention was paid to labour market factors affecting shortages than to other factors. For example, consumer market and income factors (such as fish consumption) in the different countries were completely ignored. However, indicators from four of the six major groups were selected. Many of the factors are highly correlated. For example, the industrial relations variable is constructed from working days lost to strikes. Demographic variables such as population growth were highly correlated with employment growth and could not be separately estimated. Certain politics, institutions and regulations variables, such as level of corruption in the country and intellectual property protection, were also highly correlated and only one was used. The level of intellectual property protection was chosen since it explained more of the variation in most occupations where one of the variables was relevant.

The dependent variable in the analysis is the shortage indicator constructed in Chapter 5. Because this indicator was based on sample data and because many of the detailed occupations have a small size, several dependent variables are missing in these countries.

In order to increase the value of the analysis EIU variables with no missing observations were used. Several independent variables highly correlated with one another were eliminated and indicators that are more objective were favoured.

A stepwise regression algorithm was used to screen the variables in the analysis. The variables were included if significant at the 0.05 level and eliminated if not significant at the 0.10 level when other variables were added. The variables that were included in the analysis are shown in Table 6.1 along with a description and their predicted sign. The theoretical reasons for the predicted signs are discussed in this section.

Macroeconomic indicators

Three macroeconomic indicators were related to the shortage indicators constructed in Chapter 5. Two pertain to market size and growth: EIU market opportunities and the growth of gross domestic product (GDP). It is hypothesized that to the extent that EIU market opportunities are greatest, labour shortages depend on a global rather than a national economy and would be less likely, hence a negative sign would be expected. The growth of GDP, on the other hand, is a strictly national variable. When GDP growth is high, shortages are more likely, hence a positive correlation is expected.

Net direct investment flows is more complicated to predict than either of the previous two variables. An economy with a rapidly rising GDP can give

Table 6.1 EIU indicators, their definitions and predicted signs

Series Title	Definition	Sign
I. Macroeconomic indicators		
A. Market size and growth		
EIU market opportunities rating 1997	The EIU's market opportunities rating scores countries between 1 and 10 on market size, growth rates, income levels, trading profile and natural resource endowment, with 1 being low and 10 being high	–
Real GDP (average annual growth 1995–1998)*	Percentage change in real GDP, over previous year	+
B. Foreign direct investment		
Net direct investment flows (bn US$) 1997	Net flows of direct investment derived from lines 78bed and 78bdd in the International Financial Statistics	+
II. Infrastructure (housing, transport, telecoms and energy)		
A. Telecoms & Internet		
Mobile subscribers (per 100 people) 1997	Number of mobile-phone subscribers per 100 people	+
III. Competitiveness (labour, skills and productivity)		
A. Labour costs		
Average real wages (average annual growth 1995–1998)*	Percentage change in regular weekly earnings: all full-time adult employees	+
B. Labour force		
Employment growth (average annual growth 1995–1998)*	Growth in number of people officially in employment	+

Table 6.1 EIU indicators, their definitions and predicted signs (continued)

Series Title	Definition	Sign
IV. Productivity		
EIU availability of skilled labour rating 1997	The EIU's business environment rankings quantify the attractiveness of the business environment. The availability of skilled labour rating scores countries from 1 to 5, 1 being very poor and 5 being very good	–
V. Politics, institutions and regulations		
A. Private enterprise		
Intellectual property 1997	The EIU's intellectual property rating scores countries from 1 to 5 on the protection of intellectual property, 1 being very poor and 5 being very good	–
B. Labour market		–
Industrial relations 1997	The EIU's business environment rankings quantify the attractiveness of the business environment. The industrial relations rating scores countries from 1 to 5 on the incidence of strikes, 1 being very high and 5 being very low	–
Restrictiveness of labour laws 1997	The EIU's restrictiveness of labour laws rating scores countries from 1 to 5 on the degree of restrictiveness on hiring and firing, 1 being very high and 5 being very low	–
C. Tax regime		–
Top corporate tax rate (%) 1998	Top rate of corporate tax	–
Top marginal rate of income tax (%) 1997	Top marginal rate of income tax	–

Note: *These indicators were modified for the purpose of this study and do not strictly conform to the EIU categories in which they are listed.

Source: Based on Economist Intelligence Unit (2001) (EIU) indicators. For more detailed information consult EIU. 'EIU' and 'The Economist Intelligence Unit' are registered trademarks of the Economist Intelligence Unit Limited or its licensors.

rise to income which can be invested abroad. The income growth component would be consistent with the previous shortage prediction and lead to a positive correlation. A large net direct investment could also be consistent with a country that is investing abroad because opportunities are greater due to skilled workers being more difficult to hire domestically. This too would be consistent with a positive correlation prediction.

To the extent that investors are free to invest abroad, globalization is more likely, which would predict a negative correlation. However, it is thought that this is the weakest component of the explanation and that a positive sign is most likely.

Infrastructure variables

The only infrastructure variable correlated to the shortage indicators is mobile subscribers per 100 population. To the extent that new technology has been introduced into a society, the prevalence of the infrastructure would be more likely to be positively correlated with shortage indicators.

Competitiveness

Two EIU indicators, labour costs and labour force, were converted into growth rates and correspond on a macro level to the variables used in the indicators in Chapter 5. Average real wage growth at the macro level was available in all the countries even though wage growth could be used as an indicator in only five countries at the occupational level. Employment growth at the macro level economy-wide would be expected to be highly correlated with the component employment growth rates by occupation. It was available in all countries at the national level and all but a few at the occupational level. Both variables would be expected to be positively correlated with the indicator variables.

Productivity

The productivity variable used was the EIU availability of skilled labour. This variable would be expected to be negatively correlated with the shortage indicator for skilled labour occupations since lack of supply would create shortages.

Politics, institutions and regulations

There are three different kinds of institutional variables relating to politics, institutions and regulations: private enterprise, the labour market and the tax regime.

Private enterprise

Private enterprise was tested with intellectual property. It was hypothesized that creating an atmosphere where intellectual property is protected would encourage professionals to study and stay in such countries. This would suggest a negative sign.

Labour market

The theory for including labour market variables in the model is that in countries where labour unions are strong or where labour laws are restrictive, institutions would cause barriers which make labour shortages more likely. However, these variables did not appear as significant in any of the estimated regressions. In fact the simple correlations of restrictiveness of labour laws was not even significant at the 0.05 level with any of the indicators.

The correlation of the industrial relations variable was significant in two indicators: business and administrative associate professionals and motor vehicle, locomotive, ship and mobile and plant operators and crews. However, in these two occupations other variables were more significant in explaining the dependent variable.

The industrial relations variable had a negative correlation in the two occupations, suggesting that as labour strife increases, so do shortages. However, the fact that the correlation is significant in two out of 47 possible occupations tested is not an impressive proof of this hypothesis.

Tax regime

High taxes can discourage employers from expanding business, suggesting a negative relationship between shortages and tax rates. Two tax rates were included: corporate and top marginal individual rates.

Several of the variables were transformed to correspond to the period of this analysis or to the context of this study. For example, the changes in average real wages, employment and GDP growth were computed from 1995 to 1998. By transforming the variables we also changed their meaning. For example, the level of wages is a competitiveness variable but the rate of change is a macroeconomic change variable. All other variables were measured as of 1997 if data were available, otherwise as of 1998.

While the stepwise regression method was generally followed, in a few instances where multicollinearity appeared to be a problem or the variable just barely met the 0.05 cut-off and yielded unexplainable coefficients, the final steps were not included.

Table 6.2 presents the results of the regression analysis for the nine major occupational groups. There were at least 17 observations representing countries for every major group regression. In every major occupational group the signs of the coefficients were consistent across occupations and one group of explanatory variables, top tax rates, was significant in five of the nine major occupational groups.

The remainder of this chapter deals with the significance of the variables by occupation.

LEGISLATORS, SENIOR OFFICIALS AND MANAGERS

Only one variable, net direct investment flows, was significant in explaining the labour market indicator for managers.

Net direct investment flows is positively correlated with the shortage indicator for legislators, senior officials and managers. Countries with net direct investment flows are generally countries with more rapid economic growth where shortages would be more likely. In such countries demand for managers would be even more important.

This variable explains only 33 per cent of the variation in the dependent variable as measured by the adjusted R^2. Figure 6.1 presents a scatter plot of net direct investment flows and the shortage indicator for legislators, senior officials and managers. The regression most underpredicts shortages in Australia and Italy and most overpredicts shortages in France and South Korea.

Table 6.2 Regression coefficients – summary occupations

Summary Occupations	Legislators, Senior Officials and Managers	Professionals	Technicians and Associate Professionals	Clerks	Service Workers and Shop and Market Sales Workers
Adjusted R Square	0.327	0.221	0.407	0.724	0.589
Total observations	18	19	19	19	19
Constant B (Sig.)	3.956 (0.148)**	5.371 (0.627)**	6.026 (0.764)**	2.513 (0.503)**	4.601(0.609)**
Macroeconomic indicators					
IU market opportunities rating	–	–	–	–	–
Real GDP (% change)	–	–	–	0.274 (0.061)**	–
Net direct investment flows	0.041 (0.014)**				0.023 (0.008)*
Competitiveness					
Employment growth (% change)	–	–	–	–	–
EIU availability of skilled labour rating 1997	–	-0.351 (.142)*	-0.256 (0.102)*	–	–
Politics, institutions and regulations	–				
Top corporate tax rate (%)	–	–	-0.048 (0.020)*	–	-0.065(0.018)**
Top marginal rate of income tax (%)	–	–	–	-0.032 (0.009)**	–

Notes: *Significant at the 0.05 level **Significant at the 0.01 level

Table 6.2 Regression coefficients – summary occupations (continued)

Summary Occupations	Skilled Agricultural and Fishery Workers	Craft and Related Trades Workers	Plant and Machine Operators and Assemblers	Elementary Occupations
Adjusted R Square	0.709	0.744	0.759	0.544
Total observations	18	17	17	17
Constant B (Sig.)	3.523 (0.452)**	3.447 (0.483)**	5.846 (0.549)**	1.149 (0.174)**
Macroeconomic indicators				
EIU market opportunities rating	-0.167 (0.064)*	–	–	–
Real GDP (% change)	-	–	–	–
Net direct investment flows	0.032 (0.007)**	–	–	–
Competitiveness				
Employment growth (% change)	–	0.38 (0.072)**	-	0.425 (0.095)**
EIU availability of skilled labour rating 1997	–	–	-0.454 (0.098)**	–
Politics, institutions and regulations				
Top corporate tax rate (%)	–	–	–	–
Top marginal rate of income tax (%)	–	-0.039 (0.010)**	-0.042 (0.010)**	–

Notes: *Significant at the 0.05 level **Significant at the 0.01 level

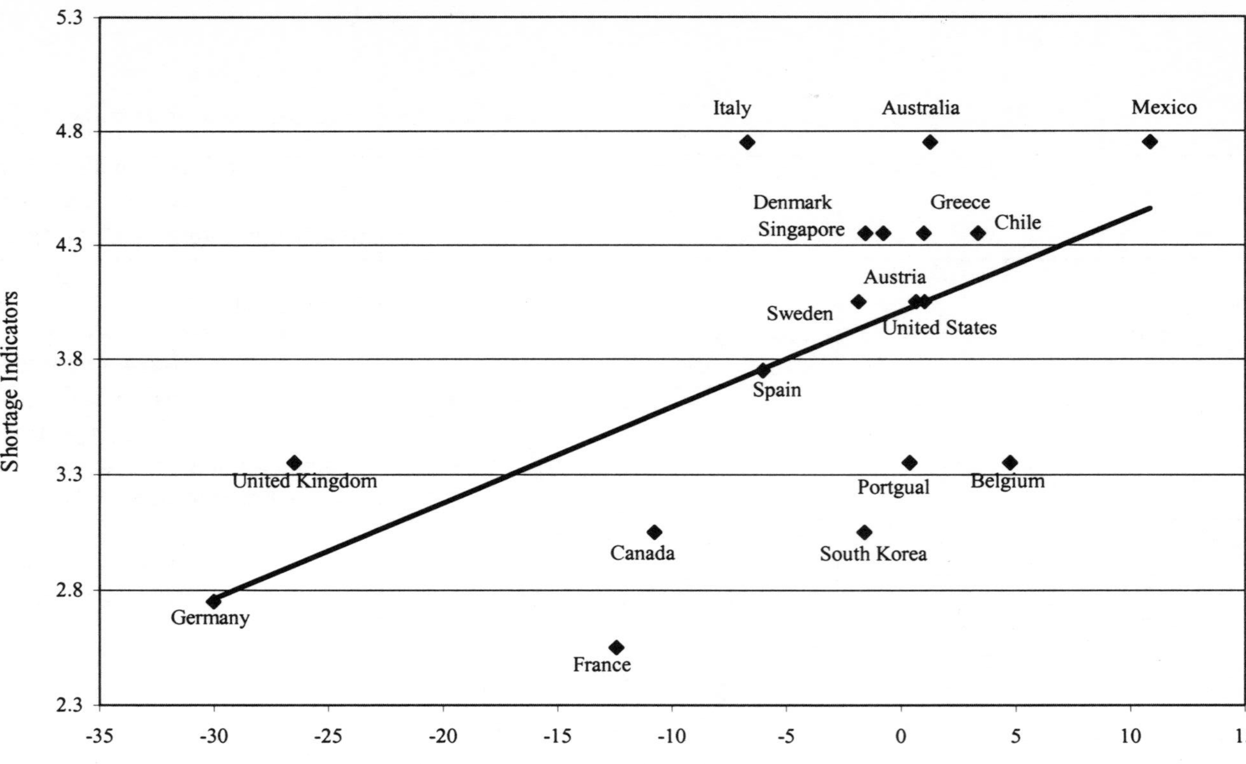

Figure 6.1 Legislators, senior officials and managers

PROFESSIONALS

The only significant variable explaining labour shortages of professionals is the EIU availability of skilled labour. It explains only 22 per cent of the variance in the professional indicator (Figure 6.2). The coefficient is negative, implying that the greater the availability of skilled labour, the less likely a shortage.

Countries can undertake policies to increase the supply of skilled labour by relaxing immigration policies, offering training and providing an environment attractive to skilled workers. The significance of this variable also validates to some degree the labour shortage indicators developed in Chapter 5.

Figure 6.2 shows the relationship between the two variables. Because the EIU availability of skilled labour variable is 5, which is the maximum value, in 12 of the 19 countries the validation is not ideal. It should be noted however that in all three of the countries where the shortage indicator is lowest (Greece, Singapore and Chile) the EIU skilled labour indicator is highest, which is consistent with expectations. Austria exhibits unexplained results with a high score in both the availability of skilled labour and the labour shortage indicator.

Some professional labour shortages, such as computing professionals, are global in origin and a country may have limited ability to influence them. When a regression was estimated using the computing professionals indicator as a dependent variable, no country-specific variables were significant. The secondary education teaching professionals regression, however, yielded two significant variables: wage changes and the EIU availability of skilled labour. Both had the expected sign. The detailed professional regressions are discussed later in the chapter.

TECHNICIANS AND ASSOCIATE PROFESSIONALS

As with professionals, the technicians and associate professionals shortage indicator is explained by the EIU availability of skilled labour. However, an additional variable, the top corporate tax rate, is significant for technicians and associate professionals.

In the regressions estimated for the nine major occupational groups, a tax variable, either personal or corporate, was significant in five of the groups. In every instance there was a negative relationship between the highest level of marginal taxes or the highest level of corporate taxes as a percentage, and the various shortage indicators. A plausible explanation is that high tax rates depress demand and consequently make excess labour

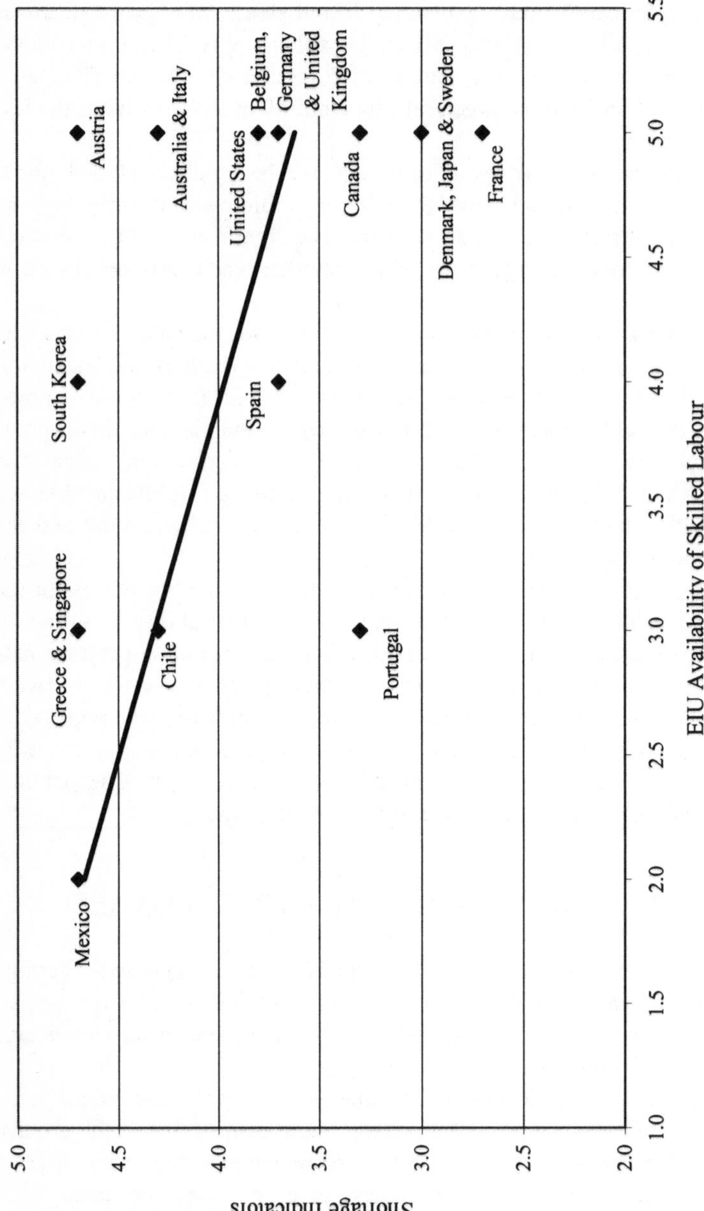

Figure 6.2 Professionals

more likely. The five major groups where a tax variable was significant included technicians and associate professionals, clerks, service workers and shop and market sales workers, craft and related trades workers and plant and machine operators and assemblers.

The two independent variables (availability of skilled labour and top corporate tax rate) explain 41 per cent of the variance in the shortage indicator.

Figure 6.3 shows standardized residuals from the regression. Residuals within plus or minus 0.5 standardized residuals are eliminated from the figure. The regression overpredicts labour shortages the most in Denmark, Mexico and Germany and underpredicts the most in Japan and Portugal.

CLERKS

For clerks, the significant variables explaining the relative shortage or surplus of clerks are the top marginal rate of income tax and the growth in real gross domestic product (GDP). The independent variables explain 72 per cent of the variance in the shortage indicator. Clerks were not in short supply in any of the 19 countries studied. Thus the indicator is explaining why some countries have more labour surpluses than other countries. The lowest possible score for this variable is 1. The variable actually fluctuates between 1 and 3.3, with only two countries having a score above 3.0.

Figure 6.4 presents residuals from the regression. The shortage indicator is most overpredicted in Italy, Austria and Australia and most underpredicted in Greece.

SERVICE WORKERS AND SHOP AND MARKET SALES WORKERS

Two variables explain 59 per cent of variation in this shortage indicator across countries: net direct investment flows and top corporation tax rate. The indicator is, on the average, slightly higher than the indicator for clerks; but like clerks the highest score for any country was 3.3, well below the range of a shortage.

The variable net foreign direct investment (FDI) flows is positively associated with shortages of service workers and shop and market sales workers. However, again because the indicator varies between 1.3 and 3.3, the variable is really explaining why some countries have surplus service workers and other countries have neither surpluses nor shortages.

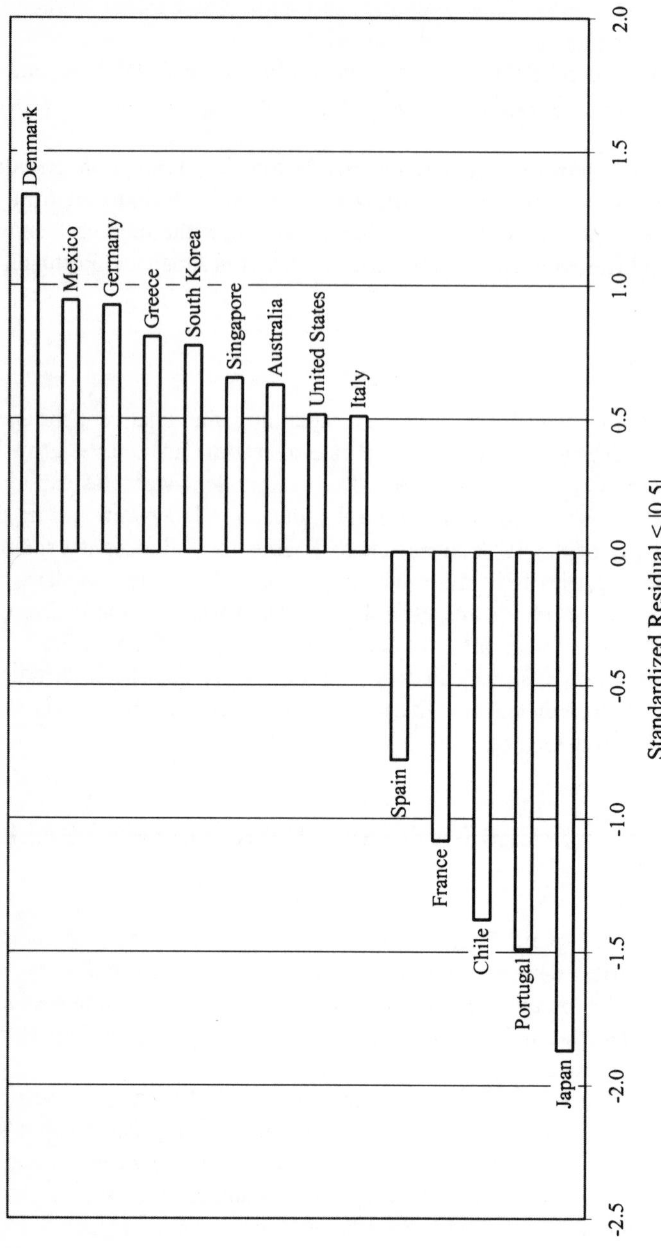

Figure 6.3 Technicians and associate professionals residuals

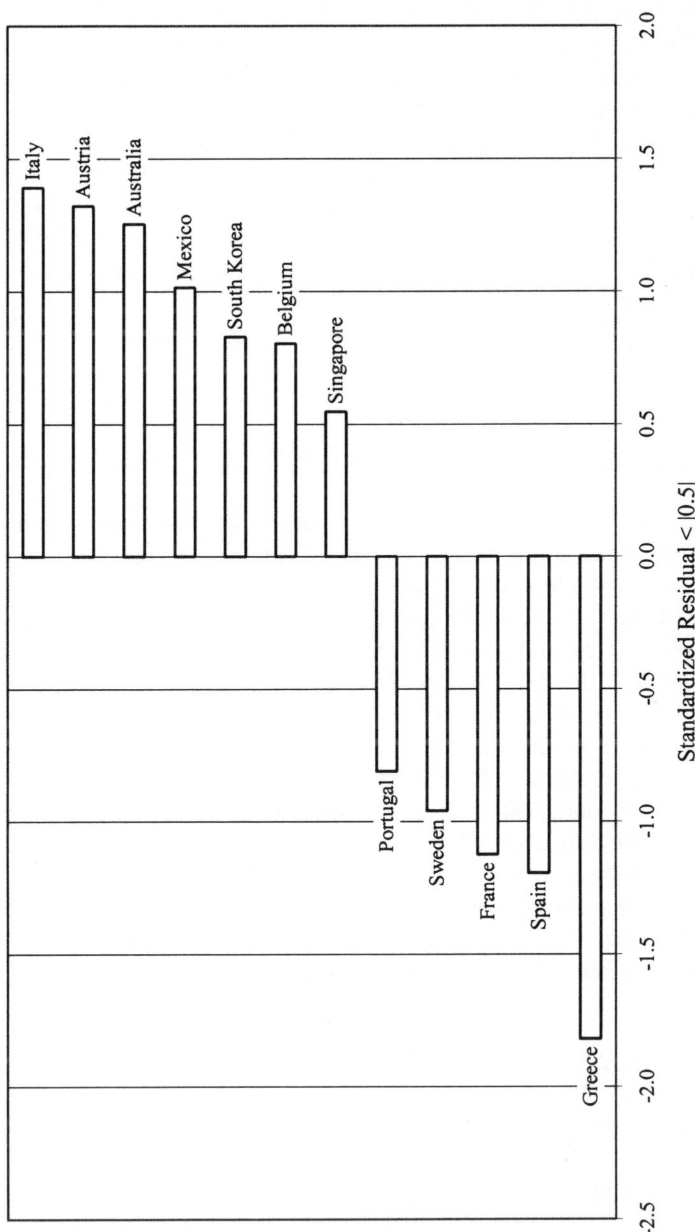

Figure 6.4 Clerks residuals

A country's net direct investment flows depend on many factors. In 1997, the year used for comparison, net direct investment flows in the United States had just turned positive after being largely negative for a number of years. In later years in the United States net direct investment flows grew substantially.

However, in 1997 the variable played a role in explaining shortages in three major occupational groups for legislators, senior officials and managers, and service workers and skilled agricultural workers and is generally correlated with economic well-being in the countries studied. The conclusion can be drawn that where net direct investment flows are large then labour surpluses were more likely.

Figure 6.5 illustrates the residuals from the regression. The regression overpredicts shortages most in Mexico and underpredicts most in Canada.

SKILLED AGRICULTURAL AND FISHERY WORKERS

Two variables, EIU market opportunities and net direct investment flows, explain 71 per cent of the variance in this indicator. Both variables have the expected sign. Shortages of skilled agricultural and fishery workers were not a problem in any of the 19 countries since the index was never over 3. The index was below 2 in only four of the countries so that skilled agricultural and fishery workers were generally neither in surplus nor shortage in the majority of countries.

EIU market opportunities measures market size, growth rates, income levels, trading profiles and natural resource endowment. It is negatively correlated with shortages. In an open economy where market opportunities are greatest, the institutions of the country must be more flexible, leading to less rigidity in the labour market and a smaller probability of shortages.

Net direct investment flows are highly positively correlated with labour shortages (surpluses) of skilled agricultural and fishery workers. Figure 6.6 presents the residuals for the regression by country.

CRAFT AND RELATED TRADES WORKERS

Craft and related trades workers exhibits a great deal of variation ranging from a low of 1.3 in Belgium and Germany, where vocational training is excellent, to a high of 4.0 in Singapore. Two variables explain 74 per cent of the variation in the craft and related trades workers shortage indicators: employment growth and the top marginal rate of income tax.

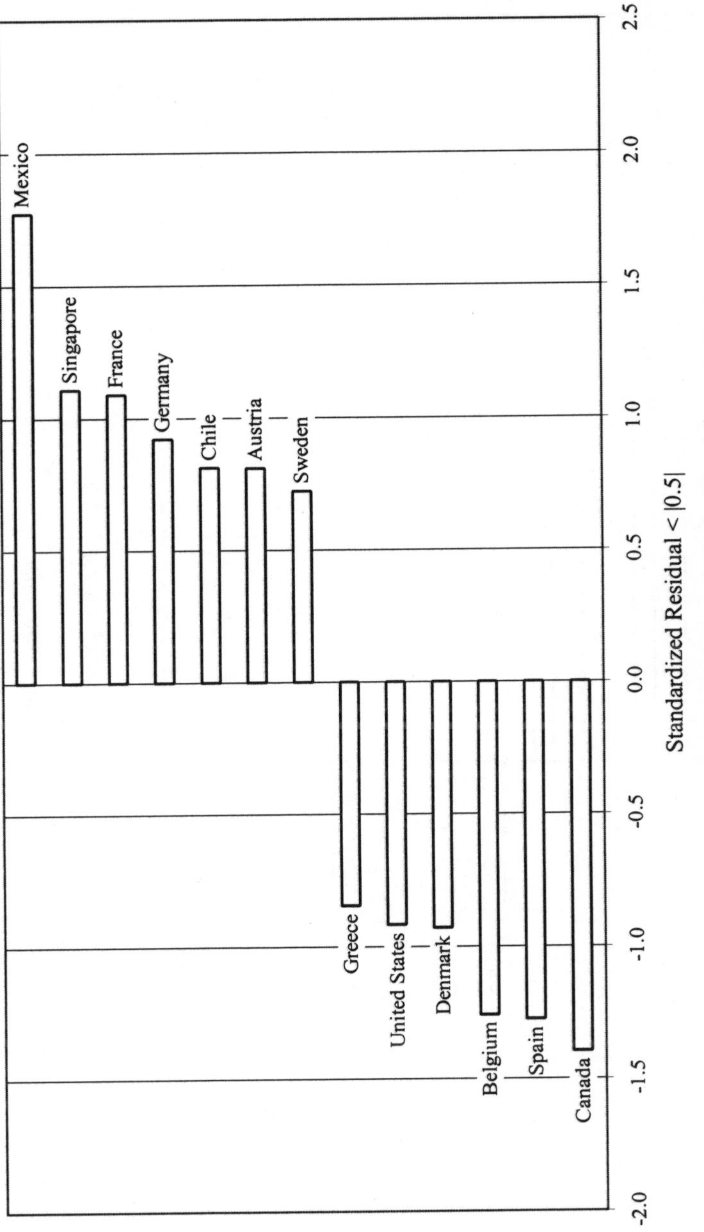

Figure 6.5 Service workers and shop and market sales workers residuals

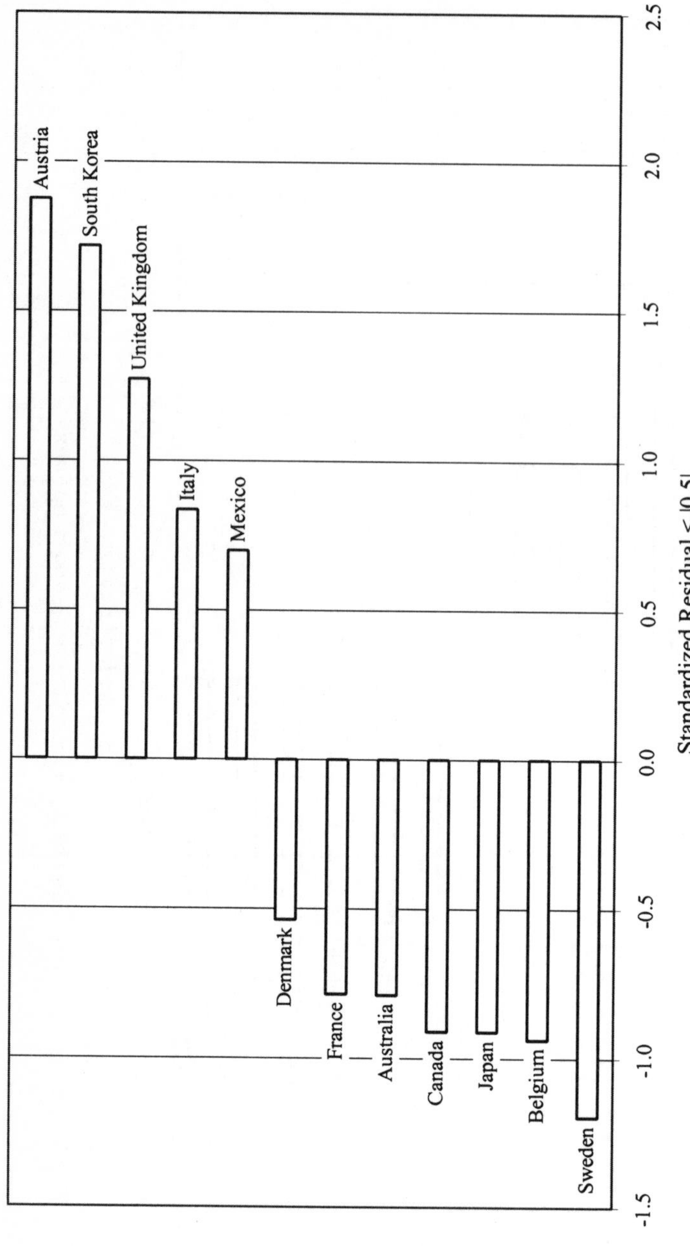

Figure 6.6 Skilled agricultural and fishery workers residuals

The overall employment growth is also significant for elementary occupations. This suggests that demand factors play a major role for blue-collar and unskilled workers but do not play so great a role in determining white-collar worker shortages.

The significance of the tax variable has been previously discussed. Residuals from the regression are shown in Figure 6.7.

PLANT AND MACHINE OPERATORS AND ASSEMBLERS

Two variables explained 76 per cent of the variance in the shortage indicator for plant and machine operators and assemblers: top marginal income tax rate and EIU availability of skilled labour.

The dependent variable shortage indicator does not involve shortages because only two countries have scores above 3.0 (and the highest score is 3.3).

The demand for this occupation depends upon manufacturing demand in a country. The top rate of personal income tax is an important explanatory variable, again having a consistent negative sign. The EIU availability of skilled labour variable has a consistent sign; however, its importance is not fully understood for a semi-skilled occupation. According to Figure 6.8, the regression significantly overpredicts the dependent variable in Australia.

ELEMENTARY OCCUPATIONS

The last of the nine summary occupations is elementary occupations. Elementary occupations include labourers in agriculture, mining, construction, manufacturing and transport as well as unskilled sales and service occupations.

Six of the 19 countries had the worst possible score, 1.0, for this occupation while two (Portugal and Mexico) had scores of 3.3.

The only significant explanatory variable was employment growth. This variable explained 54 per cent of the variance in the dependent variable. Employment growth is a proxy for aggregate demand. Where aggregate demand is weak the shortage indicator for this variable is low. The relationship between this shortage indicator and employment growth is illustrated in Figure 6.9.

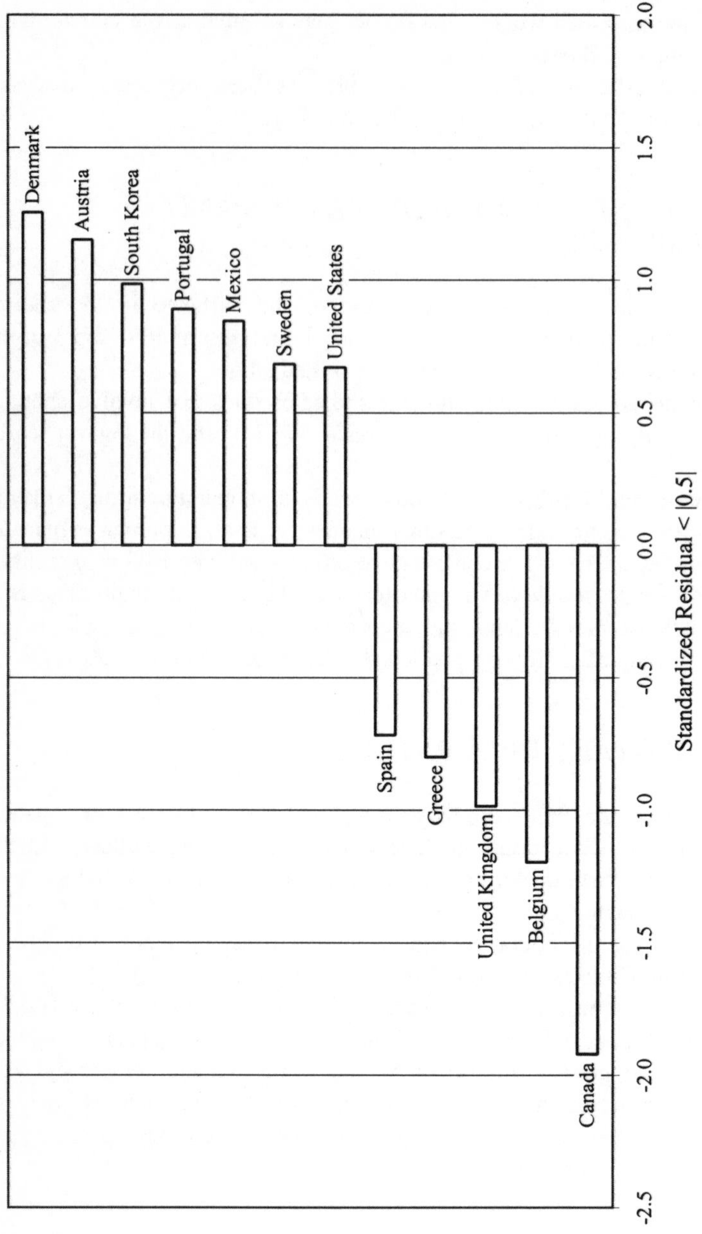

Figure 6.7 Craft and related trades workers residuals

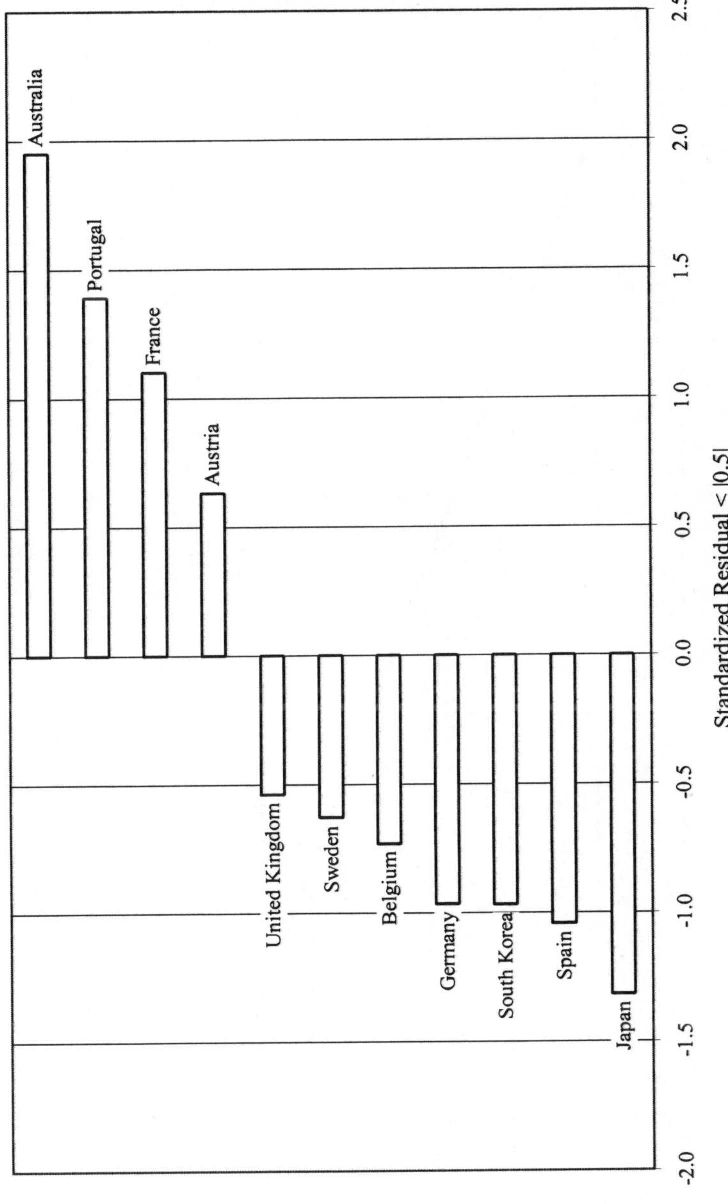

Figure 6.8 Plant and machine operators and assemblers residuals

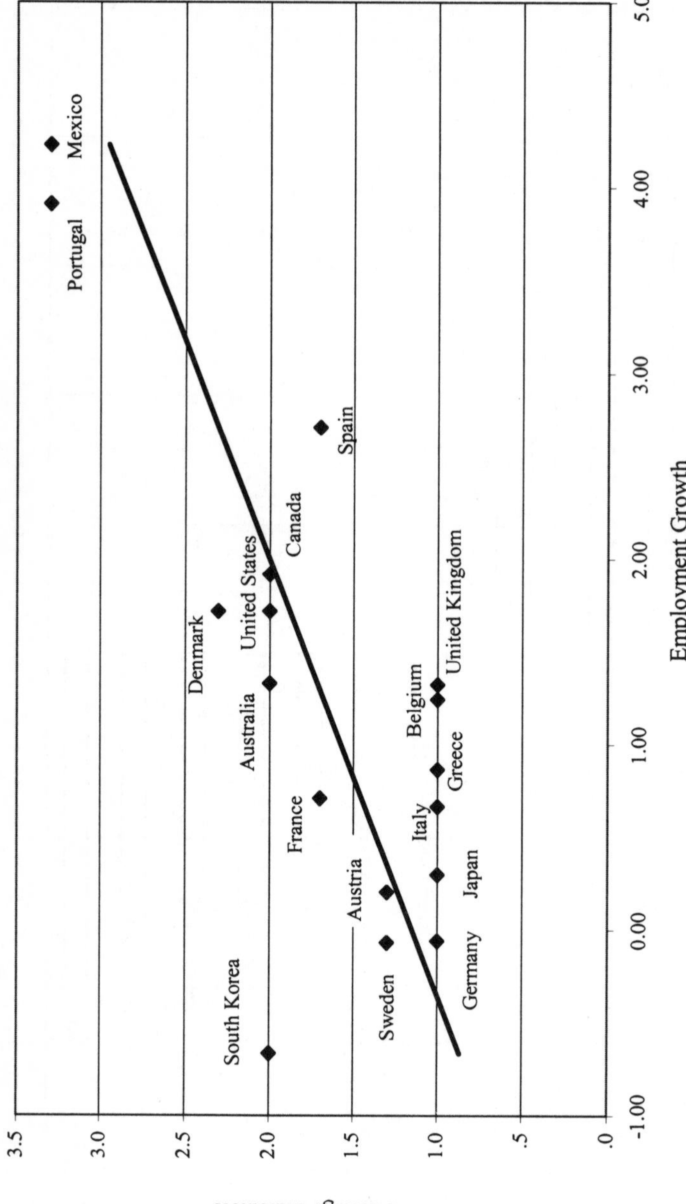

Figure 6.9 Elementary occupations

DETAILED REGRESSIONS

Regressions are shown for 15 detailed occupational groups. The dependent variable, which was being estimated, was based on data collected from a number of studies including the ILO, Eurostat and survey data from individual countries.

The number of observations varied from 9 to 15 in each regression. The dependent variable was generally constructed using survey data from the individual countries. As a rule, when fewer than 25 000 workers were in an occupation in a country, the country was excluded to prevent spurious results.

Since the number of observations was less than the summary occupational groups previously reported and the data sources were more varied, it would be surprising to find the consistency previously reported. In fact the signs for individual coefficients are not always consistent among occupations and some spurious findings are possible. Tables 6.3 to 6.8 show results of these regressions. Regressions with less than nine observations are not shown because the results were thought to be spurious. The results are organized by subgroup by occupation.

LEGISLATORS, SENIOR OFFICIALS, AND MANAGERS

Table 6.3 contrasts two managerial occupations: high level and low level. For the most senior-level managers and government officials two variables are significant: net direct investment flows and mobile subscribers (per 100 population). Net direct investment flows is a macroeconomic indicator. As previously observed it has a positive correlation with the shortage indicator. Together the two variables explain 63 per cent of the variation in the dependant variable.

The production and operations department managers indicator is also explained by the intellectual property variable. This variable was also significant for college and university and higher education teaching professionals and models, salespersons and demonstrators. Intellectual property protection is a proxy for the favourableness of the environment for private enterprise. It is a politics, institutions and regulations variable.

Intellectual property receives above-average protection in all countries in this study except Greece, Mexico, Portugal and the Republic of Korea

Table 6.3 Regression coefficients – legislators, senior officials and managers

	Government Officials, CEOs, and Senior Managers	Production and Operations Department Managers
Adjusted R Square	0.627	0.335
Observations	12	12
Constant B (Sig.)	3.635 (0.329)**	5.450 (0.973)**
Macroeconomic indicators		
Net direct investment flows	0.037 (0.012)*	–
Infrastructure		
Mobile subscribers (per 100)	0.041 (0.016)*	–
Politics, institutions and regulations		
Intellectual property	–	-0.529 (0.207)*

Notes: *Significant at the 0.05 level **Significant at the 0.01 level

where it receives only average protection. On the other hand, countries such as the United States, France, Germany, the United Kingdom and Canada have outstanding protection of intellectual property. The sign of the coefficient is once again consistent with expectations. The regression explains 34 per cent of the variance. The two variables are shown in Figure 6.10.

PROFESSIONALS

Table 6.4 presents detailed results for various professional occupations.

College, University and Higher Education Professionals

As was pointed out earlier, this occupation illustrates the negative relationship between the EIU intellectual property indicator and the skill index. The regression explains 37 per cent of the variance in the skill

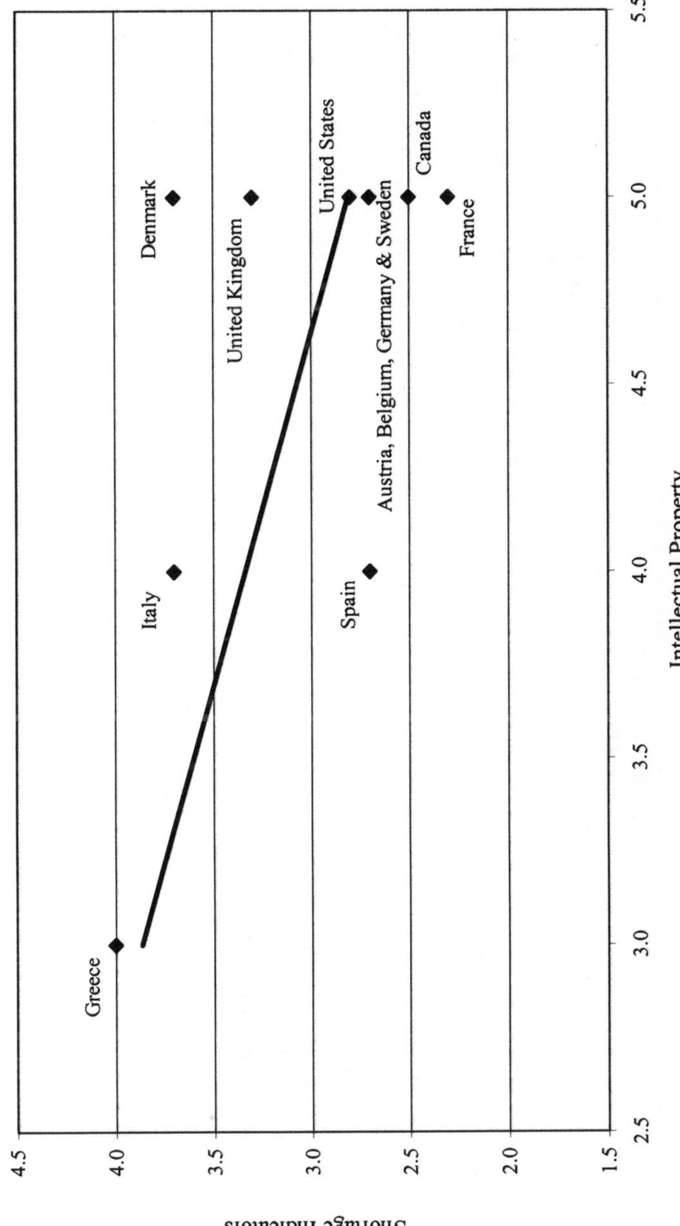

Figure 6.10 Production and operations department managers

Table 6.4 Regression coefficients – professionals

	College, University and Higher Education Teaching Professionals	Secondary Education Teaching Professionals	Writers and Creative or Performing Artists	Business Professionals
Adjusted R Square	0.371	0.82	0.437	0.285
Observations	9	13	11	12
Constant B (Sig.)	8.233 (1.831)**	5.340 (0.556)**	3.121 (0.207)**	4.437 (0.223)
Competitiveness				
Employment Growth	–	–	–	0.372 (0.160)*
Average real wages (% change)	–	0.352 (0.058)**	0.318 (0.108)*	–
EIU availability of skilled labour	–	-0.498 (0.114)**	–	–
Politics, institutions and regulations				
Intellectual property	-0.933 (0.390)*	–	–	–

Notes: *Significant at the 0.05 level **Significant at the 0.01 level

indicator. Figure 6.11 illustrates the relationship. Japan is the major country whose shortage indicator is predicted with the greatest error.

Secondary Education Teaching Professionals

Secondary education teaching professionals shortages follow expected patterns. In this equation availability of skilled labour is significant. Countries with high availability of skilled labour are less likely to have shortages. Also in countries where average wages are increasing fastest, labour shortages of secondary teachers are more likely. These two variables explain 82 per cent of the variance in the dependent variable.

Writers and Creative or Performing Artists

As with secondary education teaching professionals, the change in the average wage is a significant variable explaining the dependent variable. The variable explains 44 per cent of the variance in the dependent variable.

Business Professionals

As with the previous two indicators changes in overall average wages explain the indicator.

TECHNICIANS AND ASSOCIATE PROFESSIONALS

The three technician regressions, physical and engineering science technicians, nursing and midwifery associate professionals, and business and administrative associate professionals all have the correct signs although different variables are important.

For both the physical and engineering science technicians and the religious, artistic and social work associate professionals, the only important variable is the top marginal income tax. For nursing and midwifery associate professionals it is EIU market opportunities. For business and administrative associate professionals it is only the growth in real GDP. For all four regressions the independent variables explain about 35 to 55 per cent of the variance in the dependent variables (see Table 6.5).

The likelihood of business and administrative associate professionals experiencing a shortage is dependent on the growth of GDP in a country.

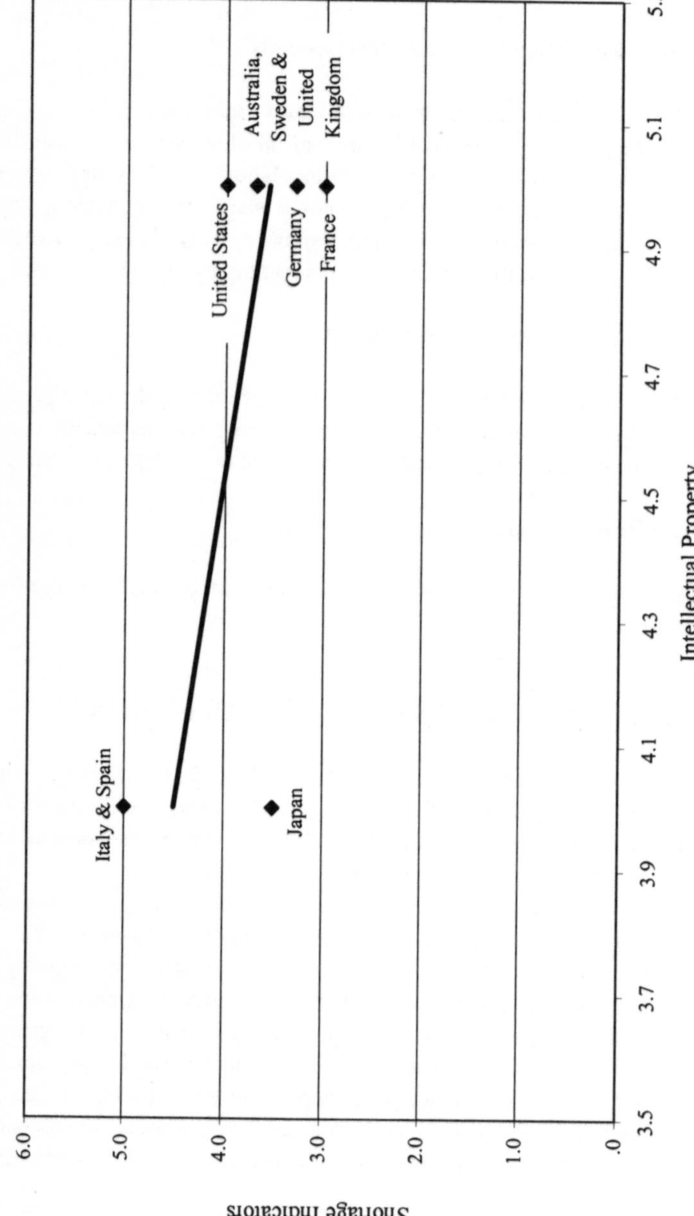

Figure 6.11 College, university and higher education teaching professionals

Table 6.5 Regression coefficients – technicians and associate professionals

	Physical and Engineering Science Technicians	Nursing and Midwifery Associate Professionals	Business and Administrative Associate Professionals	Religious, Artistic, and Social Work Associate Professionals
Adjusted R Square	0.441	0.341	0.549	0.448
Observations	14	10	15	9
Constant B (Sig.)	5.404 (0.742)**	5.22 (0.961)**	1.659 (0.357)**	5.297 (0.765)**
Macroeconomic indicators				
EIU market opportunities	–	-0.313 (0.131)*	–	–
Real GDP (% change)	–	–	0.523 (0.123)**	–
Politics, institutions and regulations				
Top marginal income rates (%)	-0.052 (0.016)**	–	–	-0.043 (0.016)*

Notes: *Significant at the 0.05 level **Significant at the 0.01 level

SERVICE WORKERS AND SHOP AND MARKET SALES WORKERS

Table 6.6 presents three service workers and shop and market sales workers regressions: housekeeping and restaurant services workers and models, salespersons and demonstrators, and protective service workers. Because the occupational groups exhibit no shortages the variables are not explaining shortages, but simply whether or not there is a surplus of workers. The signs are consistent with expectations except the tax variable for protective service workers.

CRAFT AND RELATED TRADES WORKERS

Craft and related trades workers occupations exhibit skill shortages in some countries at certain times. Three of these occupations are illustrated: extraction and building trade workers, precision and related trades workers and handicraft workers of glass, wood, textiles and printing.

Extraction and building trade workers is correlated with only the change in real GDP. Mobile subscribers and employment growth explain 65 per cent of the variance in the extraction and building trade workers shortage indicators and 56 per cent of the variance in precision and related trades workers. For handicraft workers of glass, wood, textiles and printing, employment growth explains 51 per cent of the variance (see Table 6.7).

PLANT AND MACHINE OPERATORS AND ASSEMBLERS

Both occupations depend on demand variables: employment growth in the case of stationary plant and machine operators and assemblers and GDP growth in the case of drivers and mobile plant operators. Table 6.8 shows the variables explain 34 per cent of the stationary plant and machine operators and assemblers indicator and 49 per cent in the case of drivers and mobile plant operators.

Table 6.6 Regression coefficients – service workers and shop and market sales workers

	Housekeeping and Restaurant Services Workers	Models, Salespersons and Demonstrators	Protective Service Workers
Adjusted R Square	0.441	0.579	0.229
Observations	15	14	14
Constant B (Sig.)	1.421 (0.243)**	7.096 (1.126)**	0.288 (0.953)
Competitiveness			
Average real wages (% change)	0.451 (0.130)**	–	–
Politics, institutions and regulations			
Intellectual Property	–	-0.431 (0.148)*	–
Top corporate tax rate (%)	–	-0.085 (0.022)**	–
Top marginal tax rate (%)	–	–	0.044 (0.020)*

Notes: *Significant at the 0.05 level **Significant at the 0.01 level

Table 6.7 Regression coefficients – craft and related trades workers

	Extraction and Building Trade Workers	Precision and Related Trades Workers	Handicraft Workers of Glass, Wood, Textiles and Printing
Adjusted R Square	0.648	0.569	0.509
Observations	15	15	10
Constant B (Sig.)	0.755 (0.392)	0.745 (0.360)	0.989 (0.312)*
Infrastructure			
Mobile subscribers (per 100)	0.038 (0.017)*	0.036 (0.016)*	–
Competitiveness			
Average real wages (% change)	–	–	0.611 (0.190)*
Employment growth (% change)	0.666 (0.129)**	0.513 (0.119)**	–

Notes: *Significant at the 0.05 level **Significant at the 0.01 level

Table 6.8 Regression coefficients – plant and machine operators and assemblers

	Stationary Plant and Machine Operators and Assemblers	Drivers and Mobile Plant Operators
Adjusted R Square	0.342	0.489
Observations	15	15
Constant B (Sig.)	1.159 (0.222)**	0.297 (0.437)
Macroeconomic indicators		
Real GDP (% change)	–	0.572 (0.151)**
Competitiveness		
Employment growth (% change)	0.396 (0.138)*	–

Notes: *Significant at the 0.05 level **Significant at the 0.01 level

SUMMARY

In this chapter we explored several ways of validating the indicators developed in the previous chapter and attempted to explain reasons for differences in the indicators across countries.

Labour factors such as labour–management strife measured by per capita strike activity, restrictiveness of labour laws, wage regulation and hiring of foreign nationals seemed to have no impact on explaining differences in the shortage indicators.

The important variables explaining differences in the shortages indicators were tax rates, macro variables, market opportunities and availability of skilled labour.

REFERENCES

Economist Intelligence Unit (2001), www.eiu.com, 'Country Indicators'.

International Monetary Fund (2001), International Financial Statistics, CD-Rom Washington DC.

7. Coping with skill shortages

This chapter discusses how companies have been coping with labour shortages. The success of a commercial enterprise in allocating its resources effectively is usually measured by its profitability. It is not surprising then to find that business decisions between possible alternatives are made with reference to the future. When a firm suffers from critical shortages of skilled workers (that is, when skilled workers are in high demand) it has to find ways to alleviate these shortages, first in the short term and then in the long term.

Important determinants of labour force participation are age, gender, marital status and presence of children, wage rates and labour market conditions. Some of the strategies firms can employ to cope with labour shortages in the short term are the use of overtime, flexitime, outsourcing and immigration.

OVERTIME

Overtime is the employment of a worker for more than the standard working week. A firm can respond to an increase in demand either by hiring more workers or by increasing the hours of its present employees. To avoid the cost of hiring and training new workers a firm may consider increasing the working week in the short run. This means an increase in labour costs per unit of output since the overtime hours have to be paid at premium rates. This also has implications for current, as well as potential, output.

FLEXITIME

Flexitime is when, within some limits, the employee schedules his or her own hours of work. Flexitime in some occupations can increase job attractiveness without reducing productivity. Flexitime can ease childcare problems when both parents are working. Also, improvements in information technology have made it possible for employees to work at home (that is, telecommute).

OUTSOURCING

Labour services are now becoming more mobile across countries than before. Technology permits companies to parcel out work across different time zones. For example, financial institutions in New York can send their routine computer work to India at the end of a business day and find the work completed when business resumes the next day. Similarly, software companies can outsource their software-related work to contractors in countries like Ireland and Israel without worrying about importing highly skilled workers.

IMMIGRATION

As Borjas (1999) has pointed out, immigration policies of a country often depend on whether the goals being served are those of the migrants, the domestic population or the sending country. In reality, however, most of the countries often give priority to the interests of the domestic population. Countries may want to encourage immigration to boost economic growth, to overcome bottlenecks in the labour market, to counter the aging population or to fill long-term shortages of skilled employees.[1] Job-related immigration is profitable when employers have an opportunity to recoup the benefits of investment. There are some adjustment costs, so the immigrants may earn less than domestic workers of comparable skill for the first few years.

COMPANIES COPING WITH SKILL SHORTAGES

Companies have been using all four of the strategies described above, especially in the technology industry. Companies are very concerned about the impact of skill shortages on their business expansions, maintenance of quality control and customer services. They have been using overtime but also hiring foreign workers and, in the case of the United States, senior citizens since the repeal of restrictions on the amount workers can earn before reducing social security benefits. Companies are also providing different kinds of incentives. Some examples of these include perquisites and bonuses, stock options, childcare benefits, reimbursement for tuition and textbooks, health club memberships, referral bonuses and holiday bonuses. There have been some instances where wage increases have outstripped productivity gains, but broad-based employment cost increases have remained modest and steady.[2]

Foreign workers have been playing an important role in the new economy. The high-tech industry in the US is drawing on foreign talents. It is interesting to note that Germany and Japan, countries that have been very reluctant to import skilled workers, are following the United States' example and have started recruiting highly skilled workers from abroad.

Many companies are avoiding lower standards for hiring. As Frances Fiorino (2000), a writer for *Aviation Week & Space Technology* recently pointed out, airlines 'are discovering that newly licensed, inexperienced mechanics are not transport friendly. They are deficient in the skill-sets of avionics, radio and electric, composite materials repair and computer fluency'.

Companies have increased the use of offshore talent and are not limiting themselves to development and maintenance work abroad but also 'are now farming out more sophisticated internet services' according to Julekha Dash (2000). The growth in outsourcing in most of the OECD countries is another recent trend (Murphy, 2000). Portugal has recently been attracting foreign businesses. It has been offering a 'combination of relatively low labour costs with the quality and reliability of an educated and flexible work force' (Roberts, 1999/2000). In summary, companies are doing their best to meet skill shortages in the short run by using these four strategies.

As far as the long term is concerned, firms have to focus on, and support, policies that result in an increased productive capacity of their workforce. This can be done through investment in education, job training, work experience, job search and migration. Of these, the most important is on-the-job training. Such training can be either firm-specific or more generalized. The employee and the firm share benefits and costs associated with firm-specific training, which is only valuable to one firm, as opposed to general training. Since general training is valuable in many firms, the cost of such training may be borne largely by the employee. Federal and state government taxes and subsidiary policies can also help in encouraging investment in human capital.

Many companies have been turning to educational institutions to help them increase the supply of skilled labour. Assuming businesses and governments are able, and willing, to make significant investments in education and retraining, there is still going to be a long gestation period before any increase in the supply of skilled labour is observed. As John Brandt (2000) pointed out recently, there are no quick answers to the shortage of skilled workers. What does work are two long-term approaches: investment in training and partnering with local educators.

Education and training have become economic assets. Investing in education today is what nationalization was in the 1940s and privatization was in the 1980s. The only way for rich countries to stay rich in the long term is to be more productive. This often requires better-educated workers. Global firms will increasingly take their business to countries with the best-educated workers. Many large firms have been operating in this borderless world for decades. They generally move low-skilled jobs to countries where labour is cheap, and mentally demanding jobs to countries where workers are educated.

Notes:

1. For further reading on immigration policies, see Green and Green (1999), Miller (1999), Martin and Midgley (1999) and OECD SOPEMI (1999).
2. 'Current Economic Conditions by Federal Reserve Districts' (2000).

REFERENCES

Borjas, George J. (1999), *Heaven's Door: Immigration Policy and the American Economy*, Princeton, NJ: Princeton University Press.

Brandt, John (2000), 'The Real Cure for the Skills Shortage', *Industry Week*, **249** (4), 2.

'Current Economic Conditions by Federal Reserve District', Federal Reserve System, Washington DC: January–July, 2000.

Dash, Julekha (2000), 'More Firms Seek Overseas Labor', *ComputerWorld*, 34 (17), 4.

Fiorino, Frances (2000), 'Wanted: Skilled Airline Mechanics', *Aviation Week & Space Technology*, **152** (16), 91–3.

Green, A.G. and D.A. Green (1999), 'The Economic Goals of Canada's Immigration Policy: Past and Present', *Canadian Public Policy*, **25** (4), 425–451.

Martin, Philip and E. Midgley (1999), 'Immigration to the United States', *Population Bulletin*, **54** (2), 3–44.

Miller, Paul W. (1999), 'Immigration Policy and Immigrant Quality: The Australian Points System', *American Economic Review*, **89** (2), 192–7.

Murphy, Marian (2000), OECD Observer, (219).

OECD SOPEMI (1999), 'Trends in International Migration', Paris, France: OECD Publications.

Roberts, Alison (1999/2000), 'High-tech Portugal', *Europe*, (392), 25–6.

8. Concluding remarks

> I have come to think...that although many things can be known to be complex, nothing can be known to be simple.
> – Bertrand Russell, *My Philosophical Development*

In this book we have sought to emphasize the great importance of understanding labour shortages by occupation in a global context.

Labour shortages in certain occupations have been recognized as a problem in times of expansion as well as contraction. If labour market information can be used to determine actual as well as potential labour shortages, individuals will be able to make more informed education and career choices. Such information can also guide many aspects of governmental educational, training and immigration policies.

Given the emergence of global markets and global production, we felt that it was necessary that studies of occupational shortages be global in scope. Countries seeking qualified workers have been drawing from a worldwide talent pool. Evidence of this phenomenon can be found in the immigration policies of countries experiencing worker shortages in certain occupations.

The problem of identifying labour shortages by occupations has been a slippery one for economists because labour shortages cannot be measured directly in the same way wages can be. Unfortunately there is no generally agreed upon method for measuring labour shortages. An attempt has been made here to develop a methodology which has been used to measure labour shortages in 19 countries reflecting geographic diversity as well as various stages of economic development. The *raison d'être* of our effort in this book has been an empirical analysis of occupational shortages in a global context. As was pointed out some time ago by Lord Beveridge in his farewell address as the Director of the London School of Economics, 'If, in the social sciences, we cannot yet run or fly, we ought to be content to walk or creep on all fours as infants...for economic and political theorizing not based on facts and not controlled by facts assuredly does lead nowhere' (Lord Beveridge, *Politica*, September 1937).

Some explanations for the failure of labour markets to clear have been provided. It has been shown that both short-term and long-term labour shortages can exist. Various labour market indicators have been identified and discussed as a way to solve the problem of identifying labour shortages. Four of these indicators (rate of growth of employment, unemployment rate, rate of change in wages and occupational training time required in an occupation) have been employed across 19 countries.

Standardized occupational definitions were used to compare occupational shortages across countries. The International Standard Classification of Occupations (ISCO-88) was chosen for this study.

In order to compare the performance of our labour shortage indicators for the 19 countries with other shortage indicators, we have: (1) analysed the relationship between our shortage indicators and the other shortage indicators for the 19 countries studied; (2) compared anecdotal data on skill shortages in selected countries with our indicators; and (3) studied the internal consistency of our own indicators. Labour factors such as labour–management strife measured by per capita strike activity, restrictiveness of labour laws, wage regulation and hiring of foreign nationals seemed to have no impact on explaining differences in the shortage indicators. The important variables were tax rates, macroeconomic variables, market opportunities and availability of skilled labour.

Labour economics deals essentially with the optimal utilization and allocation of human resources and rewards. Empirical data are crucial to the understanding of these phenomenon in both the developed and developing countries. It is our hope that this book will make a modest contribution to the understanding of measuring labour shortages by occupations in a global context.

Appendix:

Detailed country indicators

AUSTRALIA

Group	Occupation Title	Rank Average	Rank Training	Employment 1997	Emp Growth 1997–99	Emp Growth Rank	Avg. Unemp Rate 1997–99	Avg. Unemp Rate Rank
1	**Legislators, senior officials & managers**	**4.67**	**4**	**384**	**4.7%**	**5**	**1.7%**	**5**
2C	Computing professionals	4.33	4	141	10.0%	5	2.1%	4
2D	Architects, engineers & related professionals	3.33	4	159	-2.4%	1	1.7%	5
2F	Health professionals (except nursing)	3.00	5	77	-0.6%	1	–	–
2G	Nursing & midwifery professionals	3.67	3	205	1.7%	3	1.2%	5
2H	College, university & higher educ. teaching prof.	3.67	5	75	-1.9%	1	0.4%	5
2I	Secondary education teaching professionals	3.67	4	145	0.8%	2	1.0%	5
2J	Primary & pre-primary education teaching prof.	4.00	4	139	1.9%	3	0.8%	5
2L	Other teaching professionals	4.00	3	58	6.3%	5	3.3%	4
2M	Business professionals	4.67	4	176	7.8%	5	1.7%	5
2N	Legal professionals	3.67	5	42	-1.4%	1	0.8%	5
2P	Social sciences & related professionals	3.50	4	29	1.8%	3	–	–
2Q	Writers & creative or performing artists	4.33	4	47	6.7%	5	2.6%	4
2	**Professionals**	**4.33**	**4**	**1349**	**3.0%**	**4**	**1.3%**	**5**
3A	Physical & engineering science technicians	2.33	3	212	-2.3%	1	5.3%	3
3E	Safety & quality inspectors	3.33	2	46	4.0%	5	4.4%	3
3F	Life science technicians & related assoc. prof.	3.00	3	285	-1.2%	1	0.4%	5
3G	Modern & trad. health assoc. prof. (exc. nursing)	4.33	3	57	6.2%	5	1.1%	5
3J	Business & administrative associate professionals	4.33	3	366	5.7%	5	1.8%	5
3L	Religious, artistic, & social work associate prof.	3.67	2	108	6.6%	5	3.0%	4
3	**Technicians & associate professionals**	**3.33**	**3**	**1102**	**2.2%**	**3**	**2.3%**	**4**

AUSTRALIA (continued)

Group	Occupation Title	Rank		Employment	Emp Growth		Avg. Unemp Rate	
		Average	Training	1997	1997–99	Rank	1997–99	Rank
4	**Clerks**	**2.67**	**1**	**1156**	**1.5%**	**3**	**2.9%**	**4**
5A	Travel attendants & related workers	2.33	2	47	0.0%	1	2.2%	4
5B	Housekeeping & restaurant services workers	2.00	1	219	2.6%	3	6.6%	2
5C	Personal care & related workers	3.00	1	92	3.7%	4	3.4%	4
5D	All other personal service workers	2.33	2	42	1.2%	2	4.6%	3
5E	Protective services workers	3.00	1	94	4.0%	4	2.7%	4
5	**Service workers, shop & market sales wrkrs**	**2.33**	**1**	**514**	**2.2%**	**3**	**4.6%**	**3**
6	**Skilled agricultural & fishery workers**	**2.00**	**2**	**100**	**1.8%**	**3**	**8.5%**	**1**
7A	Extraction & building trade workers	2.67	2	272	3.8%	4	7.5%	2
7B	Precision & related trades workers	2.00	2	698	-2.2%	1	4.1%	3
7C	Handicraft wrkrs glass, wood, textiles & printing	2.33	2	119	2.1%	3	6.1%	2
7D	Food processing & related trades workers	1.67	2	109	-2.7%	1	7.8%	2
7	**Craft & related trades workers**	**2.00**	**2**	**1197**	**-0.4%**	**1**	**5.5%**	**3**
8A	Stationary plant & machine operators & assmblrs	1.67	1	180	-1.9%	1	5.8%	3
8B	Drivers & mobile plant operators	3.00	1	286	5.2%	5	5.4%	3
8	**Plant & machine operators & assemblers**	**2.33**	**1**	**466**	**2.6%**	**3**	**5.5%**	**3**
9	**Elementary occupations**	**2.00**	**1**	**917**	**2.1%**	**3**	**6.5%**	**2**

Source: Australian Bureau of Statistics. Copyright in ABS data resides with the Commonwealth of Australia. Used with permission.

Training data derived from US Dept. of Labor, *Monthly Labor Review*, November 1999.

AUSTRIA

Group	Occupation Title	Rank Avg.	Rank Training	Employment 1995	Emp Growth 1995–98	Emp Growth Rank	Avg. Unemp Rate 1996–98	Avg. Unemp Rate Rank
1A	Government officials, CEOs, senior managers	4.67	5	116	3.7%	4	1.9%	5
1B	Production & operations department managers	2.67	2	42	-1.3%	1	1.9%	5
1	**Legislators, senior officials & managers**	**4.00**	**4**	**158**	**2.4%**	**3**	**1.9%**	**5**
2F	Health professionals (except nursing)	3.67	5	37	-0.4%	1	1.2%	5
2I	Secondary education teaching professionals	3.33	4	114	-9.1%	1	0.5%	5
2J	Primary & pre-primary education teaching prof.	4.33	4	27	5.7%	5	2.2%	4
2 H-L*	(see notes)	3.33	4	149	-4.6%	1	0.6%	5
2M	Business professionals	4.33	4	13	61.4%	5	3.0%	4
2Q	Writers & creative or performing artists	2.67	4	24	1.6%	3	8.5%	1
2	**Professionals**	**4.67**	**4**	**282**	**4.2%**	**5**	**1.5%**	**5**
3A	Physical & engineering science technicians	3.33	3	105	1.9%	3	3.1%	4
3B	Computer associate professionals	3.67	3	25	13.6%	5	4.8%	3
3G	Modern & traditional health assoc. prof. (exc. nursing)	3.67	3	30	2.1%	3	1.9%	5
3H	Nursing & midwifery associate professionals	4.00	2	74	4.8%	5	1.3%	5
3I	Teaching associate professionals	2.33	1	49	-0.1%	1	0.9%	5
3J	Business & administrative associate professionals	3.00	3	110	-7.5%	1	1.8%	5
3K	Police & government inspectors & detectives	3.67	2	42	4.4%	5	2.4%	4
3L	Religious, artistic, & social work associate prof.	3.33	2	32	11.7%	5	5.4%	3
3	**Technicians & associate professionals**	**3.33**	**3**	**487**	**1.6%**	**3**	**2.5%**	**4**
4	**Clerks**	**2.00**	**1**	**520**	**-0.4%**	**1**	**3.4%**	**4**
5B	Housekeeping & restaurant services workers	3.00	1	105	6.3%	5	5.9%	3

AUSTRIA (continued)

Group	Occupation Title	Rank		Employment	Emp Growth		Avg. Unemp Rate	
		Avg.	Training	1995	1995–98	Rank	1996–98	Rank
5C	Personal care & related workers	2.33	1	47	1.4%	2	2.4%	4
5D	All other personal service workers	3.33	2	34	4.1%	5	4.1%	3
5E	Protective services workers	2.33	1	33	-3.2%	1	1.3%	5
5F	Models, salespersons & demonstrators	3.00	1	198	4.1%	5	5.3%	3
5	**Service workers & shop & market sales workers**	**2.67**	**1**	**426**	**3.8%**	**4**	**4.6%**	**3**
6	**Skilled agricultural & fishery workers**	**3.00**	**2**	**212**	**0.4%**	**2**	**0.7%**	**5**
7A	Extraction & building trade workers	1.67	2	214	-0.2%	1	6.9%	2
7B	Precision & related trades workers	2.00	2	440	-7.7%	1	4.7%	3
7C	Handicraft workers of glass, wood, textiles & printing	1.67	2	30	-2.4%	1	6.7%	2
7D	Food processing & related trades workers	2.33	2	36	-8.1%	1	3.1%	4
7	**Craft & related trades workers**	**2.00**	**2**	**720**	**-5.1%**	**1**	**5.5%**	**3**
8A	Stationary plant & machine operators & assemblers	1.67	1	169	-2.5%	1	5.2%	3
8B	Drivers & mobile plant operators	1.67	1	177	-2.8%	1	4.0%	3
8	**Plant & machine operators & assemblers**	**1.67**	**1**	**346**	**-2.6%**	**1**	**4.6%**	**3**
9	**Elementary occupations**	**1.33**	**1**	**363**	**-3.9%**	**1**	**6.3%**	**2**

Notes: *2H-L:

2H College, university & higher education teaching professionals

2I Secondary education teaching professionals

2J Primary & pre-primary education teaching professionals

2K Special education teaching professionals

2L Other teaching professionals

Source: Eurostat.

Training data derived from US Dept. of Labor, *Monthly Labor Review*, November 1999.

BELGIUM

Group	Occupation Title	Rank Average	Rank Training	Employment 1995	Emp Growth 1995–98	Emp Growth Rank	Avg. Unemp Rate 1996–98	Avg. Unemp Rate Rank
1A	Government officials, CEOs, senior managers	3.67	5	200	0.1%	2	3.5%	4
1B	Production & operations department managers	2.67	2	42	0.7%	2	3.0%	4
1	**Legislators, senior officials & managers**	**3.33**	**4**	**242**	**0.2%**	**2**	**3.4%**	**4**
2C	Computing professionals	4.67	4	39	10.7%	5	1.7%	5
2D	Architects, engineers & related professionals	3.33	4	66	-1.7%	1	1.3%	5
2F	Health professionals (except nursing)	4.67	5	52	3.0%	4	0.3%	5
2G	Nursing & midwifery professionals	3.33	3	110	0.8%	2	1.8%	5
2I	Secondary education teaching professionals	3.33	4	137	-1.0%	1	1.4%	5
2J	Primary & pre-primary education teaching prof.	4.00	4	88	1.9%	3	1.1%	5
2M	Business professionals	4.33	4	56	4.7%	5	3.0%	4
2N	Legal professionals	4.67	5	24	3.6%	4	0.7%	5
2P	Social sciences & related professionals	4.33	4	40	7.0%	5	4.0%	4
2Q	Writers & creative or performing artists	3.33	4	20	8.8%	5	11.0%	1
2	**Professionals**	**3.67**	**4**	**669**	**2.4%**	**3**	**2.1%**	**4**
3A	Physical & engineering science technicians	3.00	3	155	0.2%	2	3.7%	4
3G	Modern & trad. health assoc. prof. (exc. nursing)	2.67	3	48	-1.1%	1	2.1%	4
3I	Teaching associate professionals	1.67	1	29	0.0%	1	4.9%	3
3J	Business & administrative associate professionals	2.67	3	108	1.5%	3	6.3%	2
3	**Technicians & associate professionals**	**2.67**	**3**	**383**	**0.9%**	**2**	**4.6%**	**3**
4	**Clerks**	**1.67**	**1**	**626**	**-1.1%**	**1**	**5.5%**	**3**

BELGIUM (continued)

Group	Occupation Title	Rank Average	Rank Training	Employment 1995	Emp Growth 1995–98	Emp Growth Rank	Avg. Unemp Rate 1996–98	Avg. Unemp Rate Rank
5B	Housekeeping & restaurant services workers	2.33	1	81	4.6%	5	14.2%	1
5C	Personal care & related workers	2.33	1	53	4.6%	5	9.5%	1
5D	All other personal service workers	2.67	2	39	3.1%	4	6.6%	2
5E	Protective services workers	3.00	1	57	2.4%	3	1.7%	5
5F	Models, salespersons & demonstrators	1.33	1	145	0.5%	2	12.6%	1
5	**Service workers & shop & market sales workers**	**1.67**	**1**	**380**	**2.6%**	**3**	**10.4%**	**1**
6	**Skilled agricultural & fishery workers**	**2.33**	**2**	**95**	**-2.2%**	**1**	**2.7%**	**4**
7A	Extraction & building trade workers	1.33	2	218	-0.1%	1	8.1%	1
7B	Precision & related trades workers	1.33	2	232	-0.6%	1	8.7%	1
7D	Food processing & related trades workers	2.00	2	51	2.2%	3	8.4%	1
7	**Craft & related trades workers**	**1.33**	**2**	**522**	**-0.5%**	**1**	**8.4%**	**1**
8A	Stationary plant & machine operators & assemblers	1.33	1	168	0.3%	2	10.4%	1
8B	Drivers & mobile plant operators	1.33	1	144	-1.9%	1	6.6%	2
8	**Plant & machine operators & assemblers**	**1.00**	**1**	**312**	**-0.7%**	**1**	**8.6%**	**1**
9	**Elementary occupations**	**1.00**	**1**	**346**	**-1.4%**	**1**	**12.6%**	**1**

Source: Eurostat.

Training data derived from US Dept. of Labor, *Monthly Labor Review*, November 1999.

CANADA

Group	Occupation Title	Rank Avg.	Rank Training	Emp 1995	Emp Growth 1995–98	Emp Growth Rank	Rate 1995–98	Rate Rank	Wage Change 1997–98	Wage Change Rank
1A	Government officials, CEOs, senior managers	3.50	5	146	1.8%	3	2.0%	4	1.3%	2
1B	Production & operations department managers	2.50	2	1558	0.1%	2	3.0%	4	0.8%	2
1	**Legislators, senior officials & managers**	**3.00**	**4**	**1703**	**0.3%**	**2**	**2.9%**	**4**	**0.6%**	**2**
2 F-G [a]	(see note a)	2.75	4	401	-0.2%	1	1.3%	5	-0.6%	1
2 H-L [b]	(see note b)	2.75	4	542	0.8%	2	3.4%	4	-0.5%	1
2M	Business professionals	3.50	4	834	0.3%	2	3.8%	4	4.1%	4
2Q	Writers & creative or performing artists	3.50	4	354	4.0%	5	5.9%	3	1.4%	2
2 N-R, 3L [c]	(see note c)	4.00	4	352	4.6%	5	3.2%	4	1.8%	3
2	**Professionals**	**3.25**	**4**	**3162**	**2.7%**	**3**	**3.6%**	**4**	**1.4%**	**2**
3 F-H [d]	(see note d)	3.00	2	311	3.8%	4	2.6%	4	1.1%	2
3J	Business & administrative associate prof.	3.50	3	826	3.6%	4	3.1%	4	2.2%	3
3K, 5E [e]	(see note e)	2.67	2	195	1.8%	3	4.4%	3	0.8%	–
3	**Technicians & associate professionals**	**3.25**	**3**	**1332**	**3.4%**	**4**	**3.2%**	**4**	**0.0%**	**2**
4	**Clerks**	**2.25**	**1**	**1251**	**0.0%**	**2**	**5.5%**	**3**	**1.9%**	**3**
5B	Housekeeping & restaurant services wrkrs.	1.50	1	444	1.2%	2	9.3%	1	0.9%	2
5 C-D [f]	(see note f)	2.25	1	335	2.5%	3	7.1%	2	3.0%	3
5F	Models, salespersons & demonstrators	2.25	1	766	1.7%	3	6.7%	2	1.9%	3
5	**Service workers, shop & market sales wrkrs.**	**2.00**	**1**	**1956**	**1.8%**	**3**	**8.1%**	**1**	**1.6%**	**3**
6	**Skilled agricultural & fishery workers**	**1.50**	**2**	**595**	**0.4%**	**2**	**9.9%**	**1**	**-0.6%**	**1**
7A	Extraction & building trade workers	2.50	2	244	4.7%	5	14.0%	1	0.6%	2
7B	Precision & related trades workers	2.25	2	698	1.3%	2	6.3%	2	2.2%	3
7	**Craft & related trades workers**	**2.25**	**2**	**942**	**2.2%**	**3**	**8.5%**	**1**	**1.7%**	**3**

CANADA (continued)

Group	Occupation Title	Rank Avg.	Rank Training	ent 1995	Emp Growth 1995–98	Emp Growth Rank	Rate 1995–98	Rate Rank	Wage Change 1997–98	Wage Change Rank
8A	Stationary plant & machine oper. & assemblers	2.75	1	800	4.1%	5	7.3%	2	2.2%	3
8B	Drivers & mobile plant operators	2.00	1	519	1.3%	2	8.0%	2	2.6%	3
8	**Plant & machine operators & assemblers**	**2.50**	**1**	**1319**	**3.0%**	**4**	**7.6%**	**2**	**2.3%**	**3**
9	**Elementary occupations**	**2.00**	**1**	**482**	**4.4%**	**5**	**14.4%**	**1**	**-0.6%**	**1**

Notes:

a: 2F Health professionals (except nursing)
2G Nursing & midwifery professionals

b: 2H College, university & higher education teaching professionals
2I Secondary education teaching professionals
2J Primary & pre-primary education teaching professionals
2K Special education teaching professionals
2L Other teaching professionals

c: 2N Legal professionals
2O Archivists, librarians & related information professionals
2P Social sciences & related professionals
2Q Writers & creative or performing artists
2R Religious professionals
3L Religious, artistic, & social work associate professionals

d: 3F Life science technicians & related associate professionals
3G Modern & traditional health associate prof. (except nursing)
3H Nursing & midwifery associate professionals

e: 3K Police & government inspectors & detectives
5E Protective services workers

f: 5C Personal care & related workers
5D All other personal service workers

Source : Derived from the Statistics Canada Labour Force Survey, special tabulations.
Training data derived from US Dept. of Labor, *Monthly Labor Review*, November 1999.

CHILE

Group	Occupation Title	Rank Average	Rank Training	Employment 1995	Emp Growth 1995–98	Emp Growth Rank	Avg. Unemp Rate 1996–98	Avg. Unemp Rate Rank
1	Legislators, senior officials & managers	4.33	4	444	7.8%	5	2.1%	4
2	Professionals	4.33	4	168	3.4%	4	1.0%	5
3	Technicians & associate professionals	3.00	3	710	2.7%	4	6.8%	2
4	Clerks	2.67	1	624	3.3%	4	5.1%	3
5	Service workers & shop & market sales wrkrs	2.67	1	638	3.8%	4	5.7%	3
6	Skilled agricultural & fishery workers	2.67	2	795	0.0%	2	2.6%	4
7/8/9	Craft & related trades workers	2.00	1	1600	1.5%	3	7.0%	2
	Plant & machine operators & assemblers							
	Elementary occupations							

Source: *Yearbook of Labour Statistics* (2000), 59th Issue, Geneva: International Labour Office, 187-8, 614-5. Copyright © International Labour Organization 2001
Training data derived from US Dept. of *Labor Monthly Labor Review*, November 1999.

DENMARK

Group	Occupation Title	Rank Average	Rank Training	Employment 1995	Emp Growth 1995–98	Emp Growth Rank	Avg. Unemp Rate 1996–98	Avg. Unemp Rate Rank
1A	Government officials, CEOs, senior managers	4.67	5	54	4.2%	5	4.0%	4
1B	Production & operations department managers	3.67	2	29	8.4%	5	2.8%	4
1	**Legislators, senior officials & managers**	**4.33**	**4**	**83**	**5.7%**	**5**	**3.5%**	**4**
2D	Architects, engineers & related professionals	2.67	4	48	-0.2%	1	4.7%	3
2F	Health professionals (except nursing)	3.33	5	28	-5.8%	1	4.0%	4
2I	Secondary education teaching professionals	3.00	4	28	-4.6%	1	2.2%	4
2J	Primary & pre-primary education teaching prof.	3.33	4	72	-0.2%	1	1.3%	5
2M	Business professionals	3.00	4	45	-3.8%	1	2.5%	4
2	**Professionals**	**3.00**	**4**	**315**	**0.0%**	**1**	**2.8%**	**4**
3A	Physical & engineering science technicians	2.33	3	67	-1.3%	1	5.6%	3
3G	Modern & trad. health assoc. prof. (exc. nursing)	4.00	3	26	12.0%	5	2.5%	4
3H	Nursing & midwifery associate professionals	2.67	2	47	-2.2%	1	0.3%	5
3I	Teaching associate professionals	2.00	1	70	-0.1%	1	2.7%	4
3J	Business & administrative associate professionals	4.00	3	148	8.7%	5	3.6%	4
3L	Religious, artistic, & social work associate prof.	2.00	2	33	-2.2%	1	5.6%	3
3	**Technicians & associate professionals**	**3.67**	**3**	**435**	**3.8%**	**4**	**3.4%**	**4**
4	**Clerks**	**1.33**	**1**	**329**	**-2.1%**	**1**	**6.1%**	**2**

DENMARK (continued)

Group	Occupation Title	Rank Average	Rank Training	Employment 1995	Emp Growth 1995–98	Emp Growth Rank	Avg. Unemp Rate 1996–98	Avg. Unemp Rate Rank
5B	Housekeeping & restaurant services workers	2.33	1	37	8.4%	5	10.1%	1
5C	Personal care & related workers	2.00	1	182	2.6%	3	6.6%	2
5E	Protective services workers	3.67	1	15	20.8%	5	0.9%	5
5F	Models, salespersons & demonstrators	2.00	1	145	1.4%	3	7.5%	2
5	**Service workers & shop & market sales workers**	**2.00**	**1**	**402**	**2.6%**	**3**	**7.0%**	**2**
6	**Skilled agricultural & fishery workers**	**2.33**	**2**	**88**	**-6.6%**	**1**	**2.6%**	**4**
7A	Extraction & building trade workers	3.67	2	111	5.1%	5	3.2%	4
7B	Precision & related trades workers	2.33	2	165	-5.2%	1	3.5%	4
7	**Craft & related trades workers**	**2.33**	**2**	**307**	**-0.2%**	**1**	**3.6%**	**4**
8A	Stationary plant & machine operators & assemblers	1.00	1	115	-2.5%	1	10.1%	1
8B	Drivers & mobile plant operators	2.00	1	98	-3.4%	1	3.4%	4
8	**Plant & machine operators & assemblers**	**1.33**	**1**	**213**	**-2.9%**	**1**	**7.3%**	**2**
9	**Elementary occupations**	**2.33**	**1**	**277**	**4.8%**	**5**	**9.5%**	**1**

Source: Eurostat.
Training data derived from US Dept. of Labor, *Monthly Labor Review*, November 1999.

FRANCE

Group	Occupation Title	Rank Average	Rank Training	Employment 1995	Emp Growth 1995–98	Emp Growth Rank	Wage Change 1995–98	Wage Change Rank
1A	Government officials, CEOs, senior managers	3.00	5	805	-1.5%	1	–	–
1B	Production & operations department managers	2.33	2	546	1.6%	3	1.3%	2
1	**Legislators, senior officials & managers**	**2.50**	**4**	**1351**	**-0.2%**	**1**	–	–
2C	Computing professionals	3.33	4	180	3.1%	4	1.3%	2
2D	Architects, engineers & related professionals	3.00	4	421	0.8%	2	–	–
2F	Health professionals (except nursing)	3.50	5	317	0.7%	2	–	–
2H	College, university & higher education teaching prof.	3.00	5	96	-2.9%	1	–	–
2I	Secondary education teaching professionals	3.00	4	548	1.4%	2	–	–
2L	Other teaching professionals	4.00	3	55	7.9%	5	–	–
2N	Legal professionals	3.00	5	64	-6.5%	1	–	–
2O	Archivists, librarians & related information professionals	3.00	5	51	-0.1%	1	–	–
2P	Social sciences & related professionals	3.00	4	82	0.0%	2	–	–
2Q	Writers & creative or performing artists	3.50	4	118	2.2%	3	–	–
2	**Professionals**	**2.67**	**4**	**1997**	**0.9%**	**2**	**0.9%**	**2**
3A	Physical & engineering science technicians	2.33	3	720	0.6%	2	0.8%	2
3B	Computer associate professionals	2.00	3	109	-3.2%	1	–	–
3C	Optical & electronic equipment operators	1.50	2	33	-4.3%	1	–	–
3F	Life science technicians & related associate professionals	2.00	3	99	-0.8%	1	–	–
3G	Modern & traditional health assoc. prof. (exc. nursing)	2.50	3	159	1.1%	2	–	–
3H	Nursing & midwifery associate professionals	2.50	3	386	0.7%	2	–	–
3I	Teaching associate professionals	2.50	1	558	3.4%	4	–	–
3J	Business & administrative associate professionals	2.67	3	1072	1.5%	3	0.4%	2

FRANCE (continued)

Group	Occupation Title	Rank Average	Rank Training	Employment 1995	Emp Growth 1995–98	Emp Growth Rank	Wage Change 1995–98	Wage Change Rank
3K	Police & government inspectors & detectives	2.00	2	326	-0.4%	1	1.8%	3
3L	Religious, artistic, & social work associate prof.	3.50	2	226	4.5%	5	–	–
3	**Technicians & associate professionals**	**2.33**	**3**	**6118**	**0.9%**	**2**	**0.8%**	**2**
4	**Clerks**	**1.00**	**1**	**2202**	**-0.3%**	**1**	–	–
5A	Travel attendants & related workers	2.00	2	31	0.8%	2	–	–
5B	Housekeeping & restaurant services workers	1.50	1	481	0.4%	2	–	–
5C	Personal care & related workers	3.00	1	1102	4.2%	5	–	–
5D	All other personal service workers	1.33	2	162	-2.3%	1	-2.7%	1
5E	Protective services workers	3.00	1	101	4.9%	5	–	–
5F	Models, salespersons & demonstrators	1.67	1	747	-0.7%	1	2.0%	3
5	**Service workers & shop & market sales workers**	**2.00**	**1**	**2623**	**1.7%**	**3**	–	–
6	**Skilled agricultural & fishery workers**	**1.50**	**2**	**1113**	**-3.0%**	**1**	–	–
7A	Extraction & building trade workers	1.50	2	1216	-1.2%	1	–	–
7B	Precision & related trades workers	1.50	2	1266	-0.6%	1	–	–
7C	Handicraft workers of glass, wood, textiles & printing	1.50	2	59	-5.4%	1	–	–
7D	Food processing & related trades workers	3.00	2	216	2.8%	4	–	–
7	**Craft & related trades workers**	**1.50**	**2**	**2757**	**-0.7%**	**1**	–	–
8A	Stationary plant & machine operators & assemblers	1.50	1	1426	0.0%	2	–	–
8B	Drivers & mobile plant operators	2.00	1	849	2.1%	3	–	–
8	**Plant & machine operators & assemblers**	**1.67**	**1**	**2275**	**0.8%**	**2**	**1.3%**	**2**
9	**Elementary occupations**	**1.67**	**1**	**1641**	**1.9%**	**3**	**-6.1%**	**1**

Source: Eurostat.

Training data derived from US Dept. of Labor, *Monthly Labor Review*, November 1999.

GERMANY

Group	Occupation Title	Rank Average	Rank Training	Employment 1995	Emp Growth 1995–98	Emp Growth Rank	Avg. Unemp Rate 1996–98	Avg. Unemp Rate Rank
1A	Government officials, CEOs, senior managers	3.00	5	799	-3.3%	1	4.4%	3
1B	Production & operations department managers	2.67	2	289	0.3%	2	4.0%	4
1	**Legislators, senior officials & managers**	**2.67**	**4**	**1088**	**-2.3%**	**1**	**4.3%**	**3**
2A	Physicists, chemists & related professionals	3.00	4	71	2.3%	3	6.1%	2
2C	Computing professionals	4.33	4	144	14.4%	5	3.0%	4
2D	Architects, engineers & related professionals	3.67	4	970	4.7%	5	6.1%	2
2E	Life science professionals	4.00	5	37	7.4%	5	6.7%	2
2 F-G*	(see notes)	3.67	4	407	0.6%	2	1.9%	5
2H	College, university & higher education teaching prof.	3.33	5	126	-2.7%	1	3.4%	4
2I	Secondary education teaching professionals	3.33	4	715	1.3%	2	2.2%	4
2J	Primary & pre-primary education teaching prof.	4.00	4	118	1.9%	3	1.8%	5
2K	Special education teaching professionals	3.33	4	33	-1.0%	1	0.9%	5
2L	Other teaching professionals	3.67	3	61	9.1%	5	4.3%	3
2M	Business professionals	4.33	4	287	5.4%	5	3.5%	4
2N	Legal professionals	4.67	5	164	3.3%	4	1.9%	5
2O	Archivists, librarians & related information professionals	2.67	5	40	-5.7%	1	7.0%	2
2P	Social sciences & related professionals	4.00	4	345	5.9%	5	5.5%	3
2Q	Writers & creative or performing artists	4.00	4	185	6.3%	5	5.3%	3
2R	Religious professionals	3.33	4	52	-2.3%	1	1.1%	5

GERMANY (continued)

Group	Occupation Title	Rank Average	Rank Training	Employment 1995	Emp Growth 1995–98	Emp Growth Rank	Avg. Unemp Rate 1996–98	Avg. Unemp Rate Rank
2	**Professionals**	**3.67**	**4**	**3766**	**3.7%**	**4**	**4.0%**	**3**
3A	Physical & engineering science technicians	2.00	3	1091	-0.5%	1	7.0%	2
3B	Computer associate professionals	3.00	3	207	1.9%	3	5.5%	3
3C	Optical & electronic equipment operators	3.33	2	55	8.2%	5	4.9%	3
3D	Ship & aircraft controllers & technicians	3.67	4	36	3.3%	4	5.0%	3
3E	Safety & quality inspectors	1.33	2	188	-4.2%	1	10.3%	1
3F	Life science technicians & related associate professionals	2.33	3	125	-0.8%	1	4.7%	3
3G	Modern & traditional health assoc. prof. (exc. nursing)	4.00	3	231	5.0%	5	3.3%	4
3H	Nursing & midwifery associate professionals	2.67	2	736	1.2%	2	3.0%	4
3I	Teaching associate professionals	1.67	1	541	0.1%	2	6.7%	2
3J	Business & administrative associate professionals	2.33	3	2582	0.6%	2	6.4%	2
3K	Police & government inspectors & detectives	4.00	2	580	8.3%	5	1.9%	5
3L	Religious, artistic, & social work associate prof.	3.00	2	367	7.0%	5	7.3%	2
3	**Technicians & associate professionals**	**3.00**	**3**	**6739**	**1.6%**	**3**	**5.7%**	**3**
4	**Clerks**	**1.33**	**1**	**4701**	**-1.3%**	**1**	**7.1%**	**2**
5A	Travel attendants & related workers	2.00	2	43	-8.4%	1	4.2%	3
5B	Housekeeping & restaurant services workers	2.00	1	836	3.0%	4	11.7%	1
5C	Personal care & related workers	2.67	1	708	3.1%	4	5.1%	3
5D	All other personal service workers	2.67	2	327	2.2%	3	5.9%	3
5E	Protective services workers	2.33	1	344	0.0%	1	1.6%	5
5F	Models, salespersons & demonstrators	1.00	1	1624	-0.1%	1	9.9%	1

GERMANY (continued)

Group	Occupation Title	Rank Average	Rank Training	Employment 1995	Emp Growth 1995–98	Emp Growth Rank	Avg. Unemp Rate 1996–98	Avg. Unemp Rate Rank
5	**Service workers & shop & market sales workers**	**1.33**	**1**	**3881**	**1.3%**	**2**	**8.4%**	**1**
6	**Skilled agricultural & fishery workers**	**1.33**	**2**	**434**	**-0.6%**	**1**	**17.2%**	**1**
7A	Extraction & building trade workers	1.33	2	2812	-1.8%	1	12.0%	1
7B	Precision & related trades workers	1.33	2	3361	-0.5%	1	9.4%	1
7C	Handicraft workers of glass, wood, textiles & printing	1.33	2	258	-3.8%	1	10.0%	1
7D	Food processing & related trades workers	1.33	2	283	-2.0%	1	9.3%	1
7	**Craft & related trades workers**	**1.33**	**2**	**6714**	**-1.2%**	**1**	**10.5%**	**1**
8A	Stationary plant & machine operators & assemblers	1.00	1	1311	-0.3%	1	12.5%	1
8B	Drivers & mobile plant operators	1.00	1	1439	-1.7%	1	10.0%	1
8	**Plant & machine operators & assemblers**	**1.00**	**1**	**2750**	**-1.0%**	**1**	**11.2%**	**1**
9	**Elementary occupations**	**1.00**	**1**	**2805**	**-1.8%**	**1**	**14.2%**	**1**

Notes: * 2F Physicians & Health Professionals (exc Nurses)
2G Nurses & Midwifery Professionals

Source: Eurostat.
Training data derived from US Dept. of Labor, *Monthly Labor Review*, November 1999.

GREECE

		Rank		Employment	Emp Growth		Avg. Unemp Rate	
Group	**Occupation Title**	**Average**	**Training**	**1995**	**1995–98**	**Rank**	**1996–98**	**Rank**
1A	Government officials, CEOs, senior managers	4.33	5	350	2.2%	3	2.0%	5
1B	Production & operations department managers	4.00	2	21	17.1%	5	1.1%	5
1	**Legislators, senior officials & managers**	**4.33**	**4**	**371**	**3.2%**	**4**	**1.9%**	**5**
2D	Architects, engineers & related professionals	4.67	4	47	5.2%	5	1.7%	5
2F	Health professionals (except nursing)	4.67	5	58	4.0%	4	0.9%	5
2I	Secondary education teaching professionals	4.33	4	75	3.8%	4	1.0%	5
2J	Primary & pre-primary education teaching prof.	4.33	4	58	3.0%	4	1.4%	5
2L	Other teaching professionals	2.33	3	43	-0.2%	1	4.8%	3
2M	Business professionals	4.00	4	27	7.8%	5	4.1%	3
2N	Legal professionals	5.00	5	34	8.9%	5	0.6%	5
2	**Professionals**	**4.67**	**4**	**414**	**4.8%**	**5**	**2.0%**	**5**
3A	Physical & engineering science technicians	4.00	3	33	12.5%	5	3.3%	4
3H	Nursing & midwifery associate professionals	3.67	2	24	9.1%	5	2.1%	4
3J	Business & administrative associate professionals	3.67	3	74	12.6%	5	5.4%	3
3	**Technicians & associate professionals**	**3.67**	**3**	**215**	**8.9%**	**5**	**5.8%**	**3**
4	**Clerks**	**1.33**	**1**	**392**	**-1.2%**	**1**	**6.1%**	**2**

GREECE (continued)

Group	Occupation Title	Rank Average	Rank Training	Employment 1995	Emp Growth 1995–98	Emp Growth Rank	Avg. Unemp Rate 1996–98	Avg. Unemp Rate Rank
5B	Housekeeping & restaurant services workers	2.33	1	114	4.2%	5	10.7%	1
5C	Personal care & related workers	1.00	1	35	-2.1%	1	9.7%	1
5D	All other personal service workers	2.33	2	31	2.7%	4	9.2%	1
5E	Protective services workers	2.33	1	52	0.2%	2	2.2%	4
5F	Models, salespersons & demonstrators	2.00	1	204	2.9%	4	8.6%	1
5	**Service workers & shop & market sales workers**	**1.67**	**1**	**446**	**2.3%**	**3**	**8.6%**	**1**
6	**Skilled agricultural & fishery workers**	**2.67**	**2**	**760**	**-3.4%**	**1**	**0.5%**	**5**
7A	Extraction & building trade workers	2.67	2	256	2.6%	3	5.4%	3
7B	Precision & related trades workers	1.33	2	321	-2.9%	1	8.4%	1
7C	Handicraft workers of glass, wood, textiles & printing	1.67	2	23	-0.1%	1	7.6%	2
7D	Food processing & related trades workers	1.33	2	40	-5.7%	1	8.4%	1
7	**Craft & related trades workers**	**1.67**	**2**	**640**	**-0.7%**	**1**	**7.2%**	**2**
8A	Stationary plant & machine operators & assemblers	2.33	1	94	10.5%	5	11.5%	1
8B	Drivers & mobile plant operators	2.33	1	177	2.2%	3	4.5%	3
8	**Plant & machine operators & assemblers**	**2.67**	**1**	**271**	**5.2%**	**5**	**7.2%**	**2**
9	**Elementary occupations**	**1.00**	**1**	**243**	**-1.3%**	**1**	**9.6%**	**1**

Source : Eurostat.
Training data derived from US Dept. of Labor, *Monthly Labor Review*, November 1999.

ITALY

Group	Occupation Title	Rank Average	Rank Training	Employment 1995	Emp Growth 1995–98	Rank	Avg. Unemp 1996–98	Rank
1A	Government officials, CEOs, senior managers	5.00	5	163	17.7%	5	0.5%	5
1B	Production & operations department managers	3.67	2	60	29.8%	5	3.4%	4
1	**Legislators, senior officials & managers**	**4.67**	**4**	**223**	**21.2%**	**5**	**1.4%**	**5**
2D	Architects, engineers & related professionals	4.67	4	122	6.1%	5	0.9%	5
2E	Life science professionals	5.00	5	75	14.5%	5	1.3%	5
2F	Health professionals (except nursing)	5.00	5	235	5.5%	5	0.4%	5
2H	College, university & higher education teaching prof.	5.00	5	56	11.1%	5	0.8%	5
2I	Secondary education teaching professionals	3.33	4	525	-0.8%	1	1.6%	5
2J	Primary & pre-primary education teaching prof.	3.33	4	482	-2.2%	1	1.9%	5
2M	Business professionals	4.67	4	78	26.6%	5	1.7%	5
2N	Legal professionals	5.00	5	95	7.1%	5	0.6%	5
2Q	Writers & creative or performing artists	3.33	4	98	3.2%	4	6.4%	2
2R	Religious professionals	2.50	4	26	-16.9%	1	–	–
2	**Professionals**	**4.33**	**4**	**1856**	**3.9%**	**4**	**1.7%**	**5**
3A	Physical & engineering science technicians	3.00	3	553	-1.1%	1	1.9%	5
3B	Computer associate professionals	4.00	3	131	3.3%	4	1.2%	5
3C	Optical & electronic equipment operators	2.00	2	29	-4.8%	1	5.8%	3
3G	Modern & trad. health assoc. prof. (exc. nursing)	4.00	3	95	4.5%	5	4.0%	4
3H	Nursing & midwifery associate professionals	3.00	2	302	1.1%	2	1.3%	5
3I	Teaching associate professionals	3.67	1	77	6.3%	5	1.2%	5
3J	Business & administrative associate professionals	2.67	3	1323	-0.5%	1	3.2%	4
3K	Police & government inspectors & detectives	4.00	2	17	13.5%	5	1.5%	5

ITALY (continued)

Group	Occupation Title	Rank Average	Rank Training	Employment 1995	Emp Growth 1995–98	Emp Growth Rank	Avg. Unemp 1996–98	Avg. Unemp Rank
3L	Religious, artistic, & social work associate prof.	3.67	2	95	5.2%	5	3.6%	4
3	**Technicians & associate professionals**	**3.00**	**3**	**2653**	**0.5%**	**2**	**2.6%**	**4**
4	**Clerks**	**2.00**	**1**	**2844**	**-1.4%**	**1**	**3.3%**	**4**
5A	Travel attendants & related workers	2.67	2	13	26.2%	5	15.2%	1
5B	Housekeeping & restaurant services workers	1.00	1	703	0.0%	1	10.2%	1
5C	Personal care & related workers	2.33	1	218	3.4%	4	6.7%	2
5D	All other personal service workers	2.33	2	212	1.1%	2	4.5%	3
5E	Protective services workers	2.33	1	354	0.6%	2	2.3%	4
5F	Models, salespersons & demonstrators	1.67	1	1566	-0.9%	1	5.1%	3
5	**Service workers & shop & market sales workers**	**1.67**	**1**	**3066**	**0.1%**	**2**	**6.2%**	**2**
6	**Skilled agricultural & fishery workers**	**2.33**	**2**	**849**	**-3.7%**	**1**	**3.0%**	**4**
7A	Extraction & building trade workers	1.33	2	1130	-1.3%	1	8.7%	1
7B	Precision & related trades workers	2.00	2	2294	-1.1%	1	4.8%	3
7C	Handicraft workers of glass, wood, textiles & printing	2.00	2	232	-4.2%	1	4.6%	3
7D	Food processing & related trades workers	2.67	2	286	1.6%	3	5.5%	3
7	**Craft & related trades workers**	**1.67**	**2**	**3942**	**-1.2%**	**1**	**6.0%**	**2**
8A	Stationary plant & machine operators & assemblers	1.67	1	1133	-0.1%	1	4.3%	3
8B	Drivers & mobile plant operators	1.67	1	733	-2.7%	1	4.4%	3
8	**Plant & machine operators & assemblers**	**1.67**	**1**	**1866**	**-1.1%**	**1**	**4.3%**	**3**
9	**Elementary occupations**	**1.00**	**1**	**1891**	**-0.9%**	**1**	**12.4%**	**1**

Source: Eurostat.
Training data derived from US Dept. of Labor, *Monthly Labor Review*, November 1999.

JAPAN (Based on a sample – selected industries only)

Group	Occupation Title	Rank Average	Rank Training	Employment 1995	Emp Growth 1995–98	Emp Growth Rank	Wage Change 1995–98	Wage Change Rank
2A	Physicists, chemists & related professionals	3.33	4	41	-8.2%	1	4.8%	5
2C	Computing professionals	4.00	4	243	6.8%	5	1.6%	3
2F	Health professionals (except nursing)	2.33	5	96	-0.3%	1	-0.1%	1
2G	Nursing & midwifery professionals	3.00	3	520	2.4%	3	–	–
2H	College, university & higher education teaching prof.	3.50	5	40	0.6%	2	–	–
2I	Secondary education teaching professionals	2.67	4	122	-6.5%	1	1.7%	3
2J	Primary & pre-primary education teaching prof.	3.33	4	157	2.5%	3	2.6%	3
2	**Professionals**	3.00	4	**1257**	**2.1%**	**3**	**1.2%**	**2**
3A	Physical & engineering science technicians	3.00	3	64	-15.0%	1	26.2%	5
3B	Computer associate professionals	3.00	3	70	9.7%	5	-2.1%	1
3C	Optical & electronic equipment operators	1.67	2	24	-2.0%	1	0.3%	2
3E	Safety & quality inspectors	2.33	2	30	3.0%	4	-0.4%	1
3F	Life science technicians & related assoc. prof.	3.50	3	39	4.4%	5	1.3%	2
3G	Modern & traditional health assoc. prof. (exc. nursing)	4.00	3	49	7.5%	5	–	–
3H	Nursing & midwifery associate professionals	3.50	2	122	6.2%	5	–	–
3J	Business & administrative associate professionals	1.67	3	243	-5.8%	1	-4.2%	1
3	**Technicians & associate professionals**	**2.33**	**3**	**643**	**0.0%**	**2**	**0.6%**	**2**
4	**Clerks**	**1.33**	**1**	**113**	**-5.9%**	**1**	**1.0%**	**2**

JAPAN (Based on a sample – selected industries only – continued)

Group	Occupation Title	Rank Average	Rank Training	Employment 1995	Emp Growth 1995–98	Emp Growth Rank	Wage Change 1995–98	Wage Change Rank
5A	Travel attendants & related workers	1.67	2	217	-3.5%	1	1.3%	2
5B	Housekeeping & restaurant services workers	1.00	1	361	-2.0%	1	-0.1%	1
5D	All other personal service workers	2.67	2	37	-11.9%	1	4.6%	5
5E	Protective services workers	1.33	1	119	1.1%	2	-1.0%	1
5F	Models, salespersons & demonstrators	2.67	1	626	4.0%	4	1.4%	3
5	**Service workers & shop & market sales workers**	**1.67**	**1**	**1359**	**0.6%**	**2**	**1.4%**	**2**
6	**Skilled agricultural & fishery workers**	**1.33**	**2**	**29**	**-12.9%**	**1**	**-1.7%**	**1**
7A	Extraction & building trade workers	1.67	2	129	1.4%	2	-2.8%	1
7B	Precision & related trades workers	1.67	2	537	0.1%	2	-0.2%	1
7C	Handicraft workers of glass, wood, textiles & printing	1.33	2	215	-2.4%	1	-0.3%	1
7D	Food processing & related trades workers	2.67	2	47	10.2%	5	-2.5%	1
7	**Craft & related trades workers**	**1.67**	**2**	**929**	**0.3%**	**2**	**-0.6%**	**1**
8A	Stationary plant & machine operators & assemblers	1.00	1	1166	-4.8%	1	-0.3%	1
8B	Drivers & mobile plant operators	1.00	1	1324	-3.0%	1	-2.0%	1
8	**Plant & machine operators & assemblers**	**1.00**	**1**	**2490**	**-3.8%**	**1**	**-0.5%**	**1**
9	**Elementary occupations**	**1.00**	**1**	**220**	**-2.3%**	**1**	**-2.3%**	**1**

Source: *Basic Survey on Wage Structure 1995–1998*, Japan.
Training data derived from US Dept. of Labor, *Monthly Labor Review*, November 1999.

MEXICO

Group	Occupation Title	Rank		Employment	Emp Growth		Avg. Unemp Rate	
		Average	Training	1995	1995–98	Rank	1996–98	Rank
1	Legislators, senior officials & managers	4.67	4	711	5.2%	5	1.1%	5
2	Professionals	4.67	4	768	10.2%	5	1.7%	5
3	Technicians & associate professionals	4.33	3	3468	7.0%	5	1.6%	5
4	Clerks	3.33	1	2066	4.4%	5	3.0%	4
5	Service workers & shop & market sales workers	3.33	1	7309	4.7%	5	2.2%	4
6	Skilled agricultural & fishery workers	2.67	2	8100	-2.1%	1	0.4%	5
7	Craft & related trades workers	4.00	2	4376	6.6%	5	1.8%	5
8	Plant & machine operators & assemblers	3.33	1	2650	9.2%	5	2.2%	4
9	Elementary occupations	3.33	1	4399	7.1%	5	2.8%	4

Source: *Yearbook of Labour Statistics* (2000), 59th Issue, Geneva: International Labour Office, 191, 618. Copyright © International Labour Organization 2001

Training data derived from US Dept. of Labor, Monthly Labor Review, November 1999.

PORTUGAL

Group	Occupation Title	Rank Average	Rank Training	Employment 1995	Emp Growth 1995–98	Emp Growth Rank	Avg. Unemp Rate 1996–98	Avg. Unemp Rate Rank
1	**Legislators, senior officials & managers**	**3.33**	**4**	**337**	**-2.48%**	**1**	**0.35%**	5
2D	Architects, engineers & related professionals	3.33	4	42	-5.43%	1	1.41%	5
2	**Professionals**	**3.33**	**4**	**290**	**-1.17%**	**1**	**0.66%**	5
3A	Physical & engineering science technicians	3.00	3	50	-2.12%	1	1.49%	5
3B	Computer associate professionals	2.67	3	32	-13.76%	1	2.19%	4
3I	Teaching associate professionals	2.33	1	91	-11.25%	1	1.71%	5
3J	Business & administrative associate professionals	3.00	3	168	-8.94%	1	1.70%	5
3	**Technicians & associate professionals**	**3.00**	**3**	**472**	**-9.62%**	**1**	**1.30%**	5
4	**Clerks**	**2.00**	**1**	**482**	**-4.65%**	**1**	**2.24%**	4
5B	Housekeeping & restaurant services workers	3.00	1	150	8.52%	5	4.14%	3
5C	Personal care & related workers	3.67	1	66	8.44%	5	1.27%	5
5D	All other personal service workers	2.67	2	100	-25.78%	1	0.89%	5
5E	Protective services workers	2.00	1	60	-5.47%	1	2.18%	4
5F	Models, salespersons & demonstrators	3.33	1	217	4.59%	5	3.38%	4
5	**Service workers & shop & market sales workers**	**2.33**	**1**	**610**	**0.76%**	**2**	**2.89%**	4
6	**Skilled agricultural & fishery workers**	**2.67**	**2**	**427**	**-9.09%**	**1**	**0.53%**	5

PORTUGAL (continued)

		Rank		Employment	Emp Growth		Avg. Unemp Rate	
Group	Occupation Title	Average	Training	1995	1995–98	Rank	1996–98	Rank
7A	Extraction & building trade workers	4.00	2	260	15.21%	5	1.89%	5
7B	Precision & related trades workers	4.00	2	540	4.55%	5	1.84%	5
7C	Handicraft workers of glass, wood, textiles & printing	3.67	2	42	4.37%	5	3.25%	4
7D	Food processing & related trades workers	3.33	2	53	3.99%	4	3.62%	4
7	**Craft & related trades workers**	**3.67**	**2**	**894**	**7.84%**	**5**	**2.02%**	4
8A	Stationary plant & machine operators & assemblers	3.33	1	147	17.33%	5	2.64%	4
8B	Drivers & mobile plant operators	3.67	1	157	6.07%	5	1.36%	5
8	**Plant & machine operators & assemblers**	**3.33**	**1**	**304**	**11.81%**	**5**	**2.04%**	4
9	**Elementary occupations**	**3.33**	**1**	**432**	**11.90%**	**5**	**2.88%**	4

Source : Eurostat.
Training data derived from US Dept. of Labor, *Monthly Labor Review* , November 1999.

REPUBLIC OF KOREA

Group	Occupation Title	Rank		Employment	Emp Growth		Avg. Unemp Rate	
		Average	Training	1995	1995–98	Rank	1996–98	Rank
1	Legislators, senior officials & managers	3.00	4	524	-0.8%	1	2.1%	4
2	Professionals	4.67	4	972	4.3%	5	1.0%	5
3	Technicians & associate professionals	4.00	3	1841	4.8%	5	2.7%	4
4	Clerks	2.00	1	2520	-1.4%	1	2.8%	4
5	Service workers & shop & market sales workers	2.67	1	4485	1.8%	3	2.8%	4
6	Skilled agricultural & fishery workers	2.67	2	2382	-0.3%	1	0.2%	5
7	Craft & related trades workers	2.00	2	3227	-7.7%	1	4.5%	3
8	Plant & machine operators & assemblers	2.00	1	2187	-1.5%	1	3.1%	4
9	Elementary occupations	2.00	1	2296	-2.8%	1	4.0%	4

Source : *Yearbook of Labour Statistics* (2000), 59th Issue, Geneva: International Labour Office, 202, 628-9. Copyright © International Labour Organization 2001
Training data derived from US Dept. of Labor, *Monthly Labor Review*, November 1999.

SINGAPORE

		Rank		Employment	Emp Growth		Avg. Unemp Rate	
Group	Occupation Title	Average	Training	1995	1995–98	Rank	1996–98	Rank
1	Legislators, senior officials & managers	4.33	4	218	3.1%	4	1.1%	5
2	Professionals	4.67	4	125	11.3%	5	1.3%	5
3	Technicians & associate professionals	4.33	3	269	7.3%	5	2.0%	5
4	Clerks	3.33	1	220	8.2%	5	3.2%	4
5	Service workers & shop & market sales workers	3.33	1	210	4.0%	5	3.5%	4

Source : *Report on the Labour Force Survey of Singapore 1998*, Manpower Research and Statistics, Ministry of Manpower.
Training data derived from US Dept. of Labor, *Monthly Labor Review*, November 1999.

SPAIN

Group	Occupation Title	Rank Average	Rank Training	Employment 1995	Emp Growth 1995–98	Emp Growth Rank	Avg. Unemp Rate 1996–98	Avg. Unemp Rate Rank
1A	Government officials, CEOs, senior managers	4.00	5	787	3.1%	4	4.3%	3
1B	Production & operations department managers	2.67	2	77	2.3%	3	4.8%	3
1	**Legislators, senior officials & managers**	**3.67**	**4**	**864**	**3.0%**	**4**	**4.3%**	**3**
2C	Computing professionals	4.00	4	31	25.8%	5	5.1%	3
2D	Architects, engineers & related professionals	4.33	4	123	5.9%	5	3.8%	4
2F	Health professionals (except nursing)	4.33	5	129	7.3%	5	4.9%	3
2G	Nursing & midwifery professionals	3.33	3	112	4.0%	5	7.8%	2
2H	College, university & higher education teaching prof.	5.00	5	54	4.9%	5	1.6%	5
2I	Secondary education teaching professionals	4.00	4	137	12.7%	5	4.4%	3
2J	Primary & pre-primary education teaching prof.	3.00	4	285	1.8%	3	6.4%	2
2L	Other teaching professionals	3.00	3	31	5.6%	5	14.2%	1
2M	Business professionals	3.33	4	40	20.8%	5	9.9%	1
2N	Legal professionals	4.67	5	72	11.6%	5	2.3%	4
2P	Social sciences & related professionals	3.33	4	61	11.9%	5	10.1%	1
2Q	Writers & creative or performing artists	3.33	4	35	12.9%	5	10.1%	1
2	**Professionals**	**3.67**	**4**	**1188**	**7.8%**	**5**	**6.1%**	**2**
3A	Physical & engineering science technicians	2.67	3	93	3.9%	4	9.3%	1
3B	Computer associate professionals	3.00	3	33	12.0%	5	9.1%	1
3C	Optical & electronic equipment operators	2.67	2	26	6.5%	5	12.6%	1
3E	Safety & quality inspectors	3.00	2	23	3.4%	4	5.8%	3
3G	Modern & traditional health assoc. prof. (exc. nursing)	3.00	3	56	7.3%	5	10.8%	1
3J	Business & administrative associate professionals	3.00	3	544	10.5%	5	10.6%	1

SPAIN (continued)

Group	Occupation Title	Rank Average	Rank Training	Employment 1995	Emp Growth 1995–98	Rank	Avg. Unemp Rate 1996–98	Rank
3K	Police & government inspectors & detectives	3.33	2	22	9.0%	5	5.7%	3
3L	Religious, artistic, & social work associate prof.	2.67	2	56	14.6%	5	16.8%	1
3	**Technicians & associate professionals**	**2.67**	**3**	**2868**	**3.2%**	**4**	**9.0%**	**1**
4	**Clerks**	**1.33**	**1**	**1209**	**1.2%**	**2**	**15.2%**	**1**
5B	Housekeeping & restaurant services workers	1.33	1	491	0.1%	2	24.5%	1
5C	Personal care & related workers	2.33	1	236	6.7%	5	21.1%	1
5D	All other personal service workers	1.33	2	128	-2.7%	1	16.7%	1
5E	Protective services workers	1.67	1	204	1.6%	3	9.1%	1
5F	Models, salespersons & demonstrators	2.33	1	591	4.1%	5	19.9%	1
5	**Service workers & shop & market sales workers**	**1.67**	**1**	**1673**	**2.4%**	**3**	**20.1%**	**1**
6	**Skilled agricultural & fishery workers**	**2.00**	**2**	**849**	**-4.3%**	**1**	**6.0%**	**3**
7A	Extraction & building trade workers	2.67	2	911	4.9%	5	18.2%	1
7B	Precision & related trades workers	1.67	2	909	1.0%	2	12.5%	1
7C	Handicraft workers of glass, wood, textiles & printing	1.33	2	88	-2.8%	1	16.4%	1
7D	Food processing & related trades workers	2.00	2	174	1.5%	3	16.6%	1
7	**Craft & related trades workers**	**2.00**	**2**	**2082**	**2.6%**	**3**	**15.7%**	**1**
8A	Stationary plant & machine operators & assemblers	1.33	1	668	1.1%	2	15.8%	1
8B	Drivers & mobile plant operators	1.33	1	664	1.0%	2	10.3%	1
8	**Plant & machine operators & assemblers**	**1.33**	**1**	**1332**	**1.0%**	**2**	**13.1%**	**1**
9	**Elementary occupations**	**1.67**	**1**	**1749**	**2.5%**	**3**	**30.0%**	**1**

Source : Eurostat.
Training data derived from US Dept. of Labor, *Monthly Labor Review*, November 1999.

SWEDEN

Group	Occupation Title	Rank		Employment Growth		Wage Change	
		Average	Training	1997–98	Rank	1995–97	Rank
1A	Government officials, CEOs, senior managers	4.67	5	3.6%	4	6.3%	5
1B	Production & operations department managers	2.67	2	-0.2%	1	4.1%	5
1	**Legislators, senior officials & managers**	**4.00**	**4**	**1.9%**	**3**	**4.6%**	**5**
2C	Computing professionals	3.33	4	-9.1%	1	4.9%	5
2D	Architects, engineers & related professionals	3.00	4	-13.6%	1	3.2%	4
2F	Health professionals (except nursing)	4.00	5	13.3%	5	0.7%	2
2G	Nursing & midwifery professionals	3.00	3	-14.4%	1	8.3%	5
2H	College, university & higher education teaching prof.	3.67	5	-17.5%	1	10.3%	5
2I	Secondary education teaching professionals	4.67	4	21.6%	5	4.0%	5
2J	Primary & pre-primary education teaching prof.	3.33	4	-10.2%	1	5.0%	5
2M	Business professionals	4.00	4	8.1%	5	1.9%	3
2P	Social sciences & related professionals	4.00	4	1.7%	3	6.4%	5
2Q	Writers & creative or performing artists	4.67	4	9.0%	5	4.6%	5
2	**Professionals**	**3.00**	**4**	**-0.9%**	**1**	**3.7%**	**4**
3A	Physical & engineering science technicians	4.33	3	4.9%	5	5.2%	5
3G	Modern & trad. health assoc. prof. (exc. nursing)	3.00	3	0.7%	2	3.1%	4
3H	Nursing & midwifery associate professionals	2.67	2	0.9%	2	4.0%	4
3I	Teaching associate professionals	2.33	1	-5.1%	1	6.4%	5
3J	Business & administrative associate professionals	3.00	3	-2.2%	1	4.2%	5
3K	Police & government inspectors & detectives	2.00	2	-4.9%	–	–	–

SWEDEN (continued)

Group	Occupation Title	Rank Average	Rank Training	Employment Growth 1997–98	Employment Growth Rank	Wage Change 1995–97	Wage Change Rank
3L	Religious, artistic, & social work associate prof.	4.00	2	9.4%	5	6.5%	5
3	**Technicians & associate professionals**	**3.33**	**3**	**0.2%**	**2**	**4.2%**	**5**
4	**Clerks**	**2.00**	**1**	**-1.5%**	**1**	**3.6%**	**4**
5B	Housekeeping & restaurant services workers	3.67	1	8.2%	5	7.3%	5
5C	Personal care & related workers	2.67	1	2.0%	3	3.9%	4
5D	All other personal service workers	2.67	2	-5.0%	1	4.4%	5
5E	Protective services workers	1.00	1	-4.6%	–	–	–
5F	Models, salespersons & demonstrators	2.33	1	5.5%	5	-0.8%	1
5	**Service workers & shop & market sales workers**	**3.00**	**1**	**2.7%**	**4**	**3.4%**	**4**
6	**Skilled agricultural & fishery workers**	**2.00**	**2**	**1.3%**	–	–	–
7A	Extraction & building trade workers	2.00	2	1.3%	–	–	–
7B	Precision & related trades workers	2.00	2	2.0%	3	-29.7%	1
7	**Craft & related trades workers**	**2.67**	**2**	**1.8%**	**3**	**2.3%**	**3**
8A	Stationary plant & machine operators & assemblers	1.00	1	3.1%	–	–	–
8B	Drivers & mobile plant operators	1.00	1	-5.2%	–	–	–
8	**Plant & machine operators & assemblers**	**2.33**	**1**	**-0.1%**	**1**	**9.0%**	**5**
9	**Elementary occupations**	**1.33**	**1**	**-0.7%**	**1**	**1.4%**	**2**

Source: Eurostat.
Training data derived from US Dept. of Labor, *Monthly Labor Review*, November 1999.

UNITED KINGDOM

Group	Occupation Title	Rank Average	Rank Training	Employment 1995	Emp Growth 1995–98	Emp Growth Rank	Avg. Unemp Rate 1996–98	Avg. Unemp Rate Rank
1A	Government officials, CEOs, senior managers	3.33	5	898	-1.9%	1	3.9%	4
1B	Production & operations department managers	3.33	2	1444	2.8%	4	3.5%	4
1	**Legislators, senior officials & managers**	**3.33**	**4**	**2343**	**1.1%**	**2**	**3.6%**	**4**
2A	Physicists, chemists & related professionals	3.00	4	76	-2.5%	1	3.2%	4
2B	Mathematicians, statisticians & related prof.	4.33	5	20	13.1%	5	5.1%	3
2C	Computing professionals	4.33	4	265	12.9%	5	2.0%	4
2D	Architects, engineers & related professionals	3.67	4	624	1.5%	3	2.8%	4
2E	Life science professionals	4.67	5	55	5.8%	5	2.7%	4
2F	Health professionals (except nursing)	4.00	5	194	1.1%	2	0.7%	5
2G	Nursing & midwifery professionals	3.33	3	504	0.4%	2	1.4%	5
2H	College, university & higher educ. teaching prof.	3.67	5	245	0.5%	2	2.9%	4
2I	Secondary education teaching professionals	3.33	4	357	-0.2%	1	1.8%	5
2J	Primary & pre-primary education teaching prof.	4.33	4	329	3.2%	4	1.6%	5
2K	Special education teaching professionals	3.00	4	56	-10.1%	1	2.2%	4
2L	Other teaching professionals	4.00	3	150	12.1%	5	3.5%	4
2M	Business professionals	4.33	4	284	2.9%	4	1.9%	5
2N	Legal professionals	5.00	5	112	4.2%	5	1.2%	5
2O	Archivists, librarians & related information prof.	3.67	5	60	1.2%	2	3.1%	4
2P	Social sciences & related professionals	3.33	4	147	-4.0%	1	1.4%	5
2Q	Writers & creative or performing artists	3.33	4	185	3.4%	4	7.2%	2
2R	Religious professionals	3.00	4	46	-1.2%	1	2.0%	4
2	**Professionals**	**4.67**	**4**	**3711**	**17.4%**	**5**	**1.8%**	**5**

UNITED KINGDOM (continued)

Group	Occupation Title	Rank Average	Rank Training	Employment 1995	Emp Growth 1995–98	Rank	Avg. Unemp Rate 1996–98	Rank
3A	Physical & engineering science technicians	2.67	3	360	-6.3%	1	3.8%	4
3C	Optical & electronic equipment operators	2.00	2	91	-1.8%	1	4.4%	3
3D	Ship & aircraft controllers & technicians	4.33	4	31	4.6%	5	2.3%	4
3E	Safety & quality inspectors	3.67	2	39	9.9%	5	3.1%	4
3G	Modern & traditional health assoc. prof. (exc. nursing)	4.33	3	165	7.1%	5	1.7%	5
3H	Nursing & midwifery associate professionals	2.33	2	170	-3.5%	1	2.6%	4
3I	Teaching associate professionals	3.00	1	113	5.6%	5	5.0%	3
3J	Business & administrative associate professionals	3.33	3	766	2.8%	4	4.0%	3
3K	Police & government inspectors & detectives	3.67	2	48	4.7%	5	2.1%	4
3L	Religious, artistic, & social work associate prof.	3.33	2	336	9.8%	5	4.3%	3
3	**Technicians & associate professionals**	**3.33**	**3**	**2118**	**2.6%**	**3**	**3.7%**	**4**
4	**Clerks**	**2.00**	**1**	**4240**	**1.1%**	**2**	**4.7%**	**3**
5A	Travel attendants & related workers	2.00	2	68	-1.3%	1	5.2%	3
5B	Housekeeping & restaurant services workers	2.33	1	824	4.0%	5	8.6%	1
5C	Personal care & related workers	3.00	1	892	5.3%	5	4.7%	3
5D	All other personal service workers	1.67	2	180	-8.4%	1	6.2%	2
5E	Protective services workers	2.33	1	394	1.7%	3	5.2%	3
5F	Models, salespersons & demonstrators	2.00	1	1311	1.7%	3	7.2%	2
5	**Service workers & shop & market sales workers**	**2.00**	**1**	**3669**	**2.6%**	**3**	**6.6%**	**2**

UNITED KINGDOM (continued)

Group	Occupation Title	Rank Average	Rank Training	Employment 1995	Emp Growth 1995–98	Emp Growth Rank	Avg. Unemp Rate 1996–98	Avg. Unemp Rate Rank
6	**Skilled agricultural & fishery workers**	**1.67**	**2**	**308**	**-2.7%**	**1**	**6.8%**	**2**
7A	Extraction & building trade workers	1.67	2	1241	1.2%	2	9.0%	1
7B	Precision & related trades workers	1.67	2	1673	-0.6%	1	6.2%	2
7C	Handicraft workers of glass, wood, textiles & printing	1.67	2	217	-0.6%	1	7.2%	2
7D	Food processing & related trades workers	1.33	2	111	-2.0%	1	8.2%	1
7	**Craft & related trades workers**	**2.00**	**2**	**3242**	**0.1%**	**2**	**7.4%**	**2**
8A	Stationary plant & machine operators & assemblers	1.33	1	1184	0.5%	2	8.5%	1
8B	Drivers & mobile plant operators	1.67	1	**1001**	0.0%	2	7.1%	2
8	**Plant & machine operators & assemblers**	**1.67**	**1**	2185	**0.3%**	**2**	**7.9%**	**2**
9A	Helpers, Labourers, Cleaners & Handlers	1.00	1	2199	-0.3%	1	11.8%	1
9	**Elementary occupations**	**1.00**	**1**	**2199**	**-0.3%**	**1**	**11.8%**	**1**

Source : Eurostat.
Training data derived from US Dept. of Labor, *Monthly Labor Review*, November 1999.

UNITED STATES

Group	Occupation Title	Rank Average	Training	Emp 1995	Emp Growth 1995–98	Rank	Avg. Unemp Rate 1996–98	Rank	Wage Change 1995–98	Rank
1A	Government officials, CEOs, senior managers	4.50	5	12861	3.7%	4	2.0%	5	3.8%	4
1B	Production & operations department managers	2.75	2	8452	1.2%	2	2.3%	4	3.1%	3
1	**Legislators, senior officials & managers**	**4.00**	**4**	**21313**	**2.7%**	**4**	**2.1%**	**4**	**3.7%**	**4**
2A	Physicists, chemists & related professionals	3.50	4	282	-1.3%	1	1.8%	5	4.9%	4
2B	Mathematicians, statisticians & related prof.	5.00	5	45	13.0%	5	0.7%	5	9.6%	5
2C	Computing professionals	4.25	4	1150	13.5%	5	1.2%	5	3.1%	3
2D	Architects, engineers & related professionals	3.75	4	2095	1.8%	3	1.6%	5	3.1%	3
2E	Life science professionals	4.00	5	237	1.7%	3	1.3%	5	2.0%	3
2F	Health professionals (except nursing)	3.75	5	952	2.0%	3	0.6%	5	1.6%	2
2G	Nursing & midwifery professionals	3.25	3	1977	0.9%	2	1.4%	5	2.1%	3
2H	College, university & higher educ. teaching prof.	4.00	5	846	2.8%	4	2.7%	4	2.5%	3
2I	Secondary education teaching professionals	3.25	4	1232	-0.2%	1	1.3%	5	3.0%	3
2J	Primary & pre-primary education teaching prof.	4.00	4	2236	4.3%	5	2.2%	4	2.5%	3
2K	Special education teaching professionals	4.50	4	311	7.0%	5	1.5%	5	4.0%	4
2L	Other teaching professionals	3.75	3	729	4.0%	4	3.8%	4	4.4%	4
2M	Business professionals	3.75	4	3587	3.2%	4	2.1%	4	2.0%	3
2N	Legal professionals	3.75	5	927	0.9%	2	1.0%	5	2.4%	3
2O	Archivists, librarians & related information prof.	4.50	5	211	3.8%	4	1.7%	5	3.8%	4

UNITED STATES (continued)

Group	Occupation Title	Rank		Emp	Emp Growth		Avg. Unemp Rate		Wage Change	
		Average	Training	1995	1995–98	Rank	1996–98	Rank	1995–98	Rank
2P	Social sciences & related professionals	3.50	4	1526	0.3%	2	2.5%	4	3.6%	4
2Q	Writers & creative or performing artists	3.75	4	1919	4.7%	5	4.4%	3	2.8%	3
2R	Religious professionals	3.75	4	466	-1.4%	1	1.0%	5	6.7%	5
2	**Professionals**	**4.00**	**4**	**22723**	**2.8%**	**4**	**1.9%**	**5**	**2.8%**	**3**
3A	Physical & engineering science technicians	3.50	3	900	3.0%	4	2.7%	4	2.3%	3
3B	Computer associate professionals	3.00	3	1043	-1.8%	1	2.3%	4	4.5%	4
3C	Optical & electronic equipment operators	3.50	2	260	5.5%	5	3.9%	4	2.5%	3
3D	Ship & aircraft controllers & technicians	3.75	4	144	-1.2%	1	1.3%	5	12.5%	5
3E	Safety & quality inspectors	3.00	2	303	0.4%	2	2.4%	4	3.5%	4
3F	Life science technicians & related assoc. prof.	2.75	3	276	1.1%	2	3.1%	4	0.7%	2
3G	Modern & trad. health assoc. prof. (exc. nursing)	3.75	3	2088	3.1%	4	1.9%	5	2.8%	3
3H	Nursing & midwifery associate professionals	2.50	2	399	-1.5%	1	2.6%	4	2.1%	3
3I	Teaching associate professionals	2.50	1	634	-0.1%	1	3.6%	4	4.1%	4
3J	Business & administrative associate professionals	3.50	3	2547	3.5%	4	2.3%	4	3.0%	3
3K	Police & government inspectors & detectives	3.75	2	670	4.4%	5	0.9%	5	2.9%	3
3	**Technicians & associate professionals**	**3.25**	**3**	**9264**	**2.2%**	**3**	**2.3%**	**4**	**3.2%**	**3**
4	**Clerks**	**2.25**	**1**	**16556**	**0.3%**	**2**	**4.0%**	**3**	**2.9%**	**3**

UNITED STATES (continued)

Group	Occupation Title	Rank Average	Rank Training	Emp 1995	Emp Growth 1995–98	Emp Growth Rank	Avg. Unemp Rate 1996–98	Avg. Unemp Rate Rank	Wage Change 1995–98	Wage Change Rank
5A	Travel attendants & related workers	2.50	2	620	2.7%	3	6.7%	2	2.3%	3
5B	Housekeeping & restaurant services workers	2.25	1	5418	1.4%	3	8.8%	1	3.9%	4
5C	Personal care & related workers	2.75	1	3534	2.0%	3	5.6%	3	3.8%	4
5D	All other personal service workers	2.75	2	837	-0.3%	1	2.8%	4	3.6%	4
5E	Protective services workers	2.75	1	1373	1.6%	3	5.4%	3	3.9%	4
5F	Models, salespersons & demonstrators	2.00	1	8812	1.2%	2	6.8%	2	2.7%	3
5	**Service workers & shop & market sales wkrs**	**2.00**	**1**	**20594**	**1.4%**	**2**	**6.9%**	**2**	**3.3%**	**3**
6	**Skilled agricultural & fishery workers**	**2.00**	**2**	**3642**	**-1.3%**	**1**	**7.1%**	**2**	**1.7%**	**3**
7A	Extraction & building trade workers	2.75	2	4545	3.3%	4	7.5%	2	2.9%	3
7B	Precision & related trades workers	3.00	2	5537	2.2%	3	3.5%	4	3.4%	3
7D	Food processing & related trades workers	3.00	2	550	1.7%	3	4.9%	3	4.2%	4
7	**Craft & related trades workers**	**2.75**	**2**	**10647**	**2.6%**	**3**	**5.3%**	**3**	**3.3%**	**3**
8A	Stationary plant & machine oper. & assemblers	1.75	1	8499	-0.4%	1	6.6%	2	3.3%	3
8B	Drivers & mobile plant operators	2.25	1	5070	1.2%	2	5.2%	3	2.7%	3
8	**Plant & machine operators & assemblers**	**2.00**	**1**	**13569**	**0.2%**	**2**	**6.0%**	**2**	**3.0%**	**3**
9	**Elementary occupations**	**2.00**	**1**	**8564**	**1.2%**	**2**	**9.5%**	**1**	**3.6%**	**4**

Source : US Bureau of Labor Statistics.

Training data derived from US Dept. of Labor, *Monthly Labor Review*, November 1999.

Index

Abraham, Katharine G., 9, 10, 14, 33, 34
Akerlof, George, 7, 14
anecdotal validation, 49
Arndt, Sven, 21, 23
Arrow, Kenneth J., 5, 14
Australia, 2, 16, 17, 18, 19, 25, 34, 35, 36, 38, 46, 47, 50, 51, 52, 53, 54, 55, 65, 71, 77, 99
Austria, 2, 18, 19, 38, 46, 47, 50, 51, 53, 54, 55, 69, 71, 101

Barnow, B., 15
barriers to mobility, 4, 8, 9
Belgium, 2, 18, 19, 26, 35, 38, 46, 47, 50, 51, 54, 55, 74, 103
birth rate, 28
Blanchard, Oliver J., 10, 14
Blank, David M., 6, 14
Bloomberg, 30, 34
Booth, Alison, 4, 13, 14
Borjas, 93, 95
Bosworth, Derek, 4, 5, 13, 14, 31, 34
bottlenecks, 2, 33, 93
Boyd, G., 23
brain circulation, 16, 23
brain drain, 16, 26
Brandt, John, 94
Brewer, Thomas L., 23
Brownlee, Patrick, 34
business cycle, 10, 37

Canada, 2, 15, 16, 18, 19, 26, 34, 38, 47, 49, 50, 51, 54, 55, 57, 58, 74, 82, 95, 105
capital outflows and inflows, 18
Capron, W., 5, 14
Card, David, 22, 23
Chasanov, A., 15
Chile, 2, 18, 19, 27, 38, 47, 49, 54, 55, 69, 107
Clinton, A., 30, 34
Cohen, Malcolm S., 10, 11, 13, 14, 37, 49, 52, 57, 58
College, University and Higher Education Professionals, 82
commodity trade, 17
competitiveness, 59, 61, 63, 66, 67, 84, 89, 90, 91
consumer markets and income, 59
craft and related trade workers, 74, 88
Crequer, Ngaio, 32, 34
Cronbach's Alpha, 53, 55, 56, 57
Current Population Survey, 42, 58

Dash, 94
Dawly, H., 26, 33, 34
Dawson, Chester, 28, 29, 34
DeCloet, Derek, 26, 34
demographics and health, 59
Denmark, 2, 18, 19, 38, 46, 47, 49, 50, 51, 54, 55, 71, 108
Diamond, P., 10, 14
Dicks-Mireaux, L., 9, 14
Dow, J.C.R., 9, 14
Driffield, Nigel, 21, 23
Düll, Nicola, 28, 34
Dutton, P., 14, 31, 34
dynamic shortages, 5

economic growth, 1, 28, 29, 33, 93
Economist Intelligence Unit, 59, 62, 91
education, 13, 27, 28, 30, 31, 38, 40, 50, 52, 69, 81, 85, 94, 95, 96
educational institutions, 94
efficiency wage theory, 7
EIU business environment rating, 59
EIU market opportunities rating, 61, 65, 66, 67
elementary occupations, 77
Elias, Peter, 38, 58
employment change, 12, 42, 97
Erickson, Christopher L., 1, 3
Eurostat, 3, 38, 39, 43, 57, 81
Evans, 27
Ewing, Jack, 26, 33, 34

factors, 4, 5, 59
Feldstein, Martin, 1, 3
financing, 59
Fiorino, Frances, 31, 34, 94, 95
flexitime, 92
foreign direct investment (FDI), 18, 71
foreign trade and exchange, 59

foreign workers, 94
France, 2, 18, 19, 38, 46, 47, 50, 51, 54, 55, 56, 57, 65, 82, 95, 110
frictional unemployment, 12, 43
Friedberg, Rachel, 22, 23

Gallaway, Lowell E., 8, 14
Gaston, Noel, 22, 23
Germany, 2, 18, 19, 21, 22, 27, 28, 34, 38, 46, 47, 50, 51, 52, 53, 54, 55, 71, 74, 82, 94, 112
Gingras, Yves, 26, 34
globalization, 2, 16, 20, 22, 27
Gosejacob, 28
government forecasts of future demand, 13
government household surveys, 36
Greece, 2, 18, 19, 28, 38, 46, 47, 49, 50, 51, 54, 55, 69, 71, 81, 115
green card initiative, 28
Green, A.G., 95
Green, D.A., 95
Greenaway, David, 22, 23
gross domestic product, 1, 60, 71
Guth, Rob, 25, 34

Hall, Robert, 11, 14
Ham, H., 53, 58
Haney, C., 34
Hatch, Julie, 30, 34
Heijke, Hans, 35
help-wanted ads, 10
help-wanted advertising, 10, 12
help-wanted index, 10
high tech industry, 94
hiring transactions, 11

immigration policies, 16, 69, 93, 95, 96
Inagami, Takeshi, 29, 30, 35
incentives, 4, 16, 93
indicator, 11, 37, 42, 46, 49, 69, 71
industrial relations, 53, 59, 60, 62, 64
information technology, 25, 32, 92
infrastructure, 59, 61, 63, 82, 90
insider – outsider, 7
institutional barriers, 53
intellectual property, 60, 62, 64, 81, 82
internal consistency, 36, 52, 53, 97
internal labour market, 31
International Labour Organization, 35, 38, 39
International Monetary Fund, 91
International Standard Classification of Occupations (ISCO), 38, 97
Italy, 2, 18, 19, 38, 46, 47, 49, 50, 51, 53, 54, 55, 65, 71, 117

Japan, 2, 17, 18, 19, 28, 29, 34, 38, 46, 47, 50, 51, 54, 55, 71, 85, 94, 119
Jeong, Jooyeon, 30, 35
job vacancies, 9, 37
Jorgenson, Dale W., 20, 23

Kimbell, L., 1, 3
Kleiner, Morris M., 53, 58

labour certifications, 13
labour costs, 29, 61
labour demand, 1, 4, 6, 9, 33, 37
labour economics, 97
labour force participation, 92
labour market, 5, 6, 8, 9, 12, 13, 35, 37, 42, 59, 62, 64, 92
labour mobility, 8
labour shortage indicators, 2, 25, 69, 97
labour shortages, 1, 2, 5, 6, 9, 11, 12, 13, 16, 25, 26, 28, 31, 33, 35, 36, 37, 49, 53, 69, 71, 74, 85, 92, 96, 97
labour supply, 4, 42, 53
labour turnover, 11
Legard, D., 34
legislators, 65, 81
level of training requirements, 13
Lewis, J., 14, 31, 34
Lindbeck, Assar, 7, 14
Lord Beveridge, 96
Lynch, Lisa M., 33, 35

macroeconomic indicators, 59, 60, 61, 67, 82, 87, 91
managers, 65, 81
Martin, Philip, 95
Mexico, 2, 18, 19, 38, 46, 47, 49, 54, 55, 71, 74, 77, 81, 121
Midgley, E., 95
Miller, Paul W., 95
Mitchell, C, 34
Mitchell, D.J.B., 1, 3
multicollinearity, 65

Murphy, Marian, 23, 94, 95
Muysken, J., 4, 14

Nelson, D., 22, 23
net direct investment, 63, 65, 71, 74, 81
new hires, 9, 10, 11, 12
Nomuva, Makoto, 29

occupation, 1, 2, 4, 7, 8, 9, 12, 13, 33, 36, 37, 38, 39, 42, 43, 44, 45, 46, 49, 52, 53, 57, 65, 77, 81, 82, 96, 97
Occupational Employment Survey, 39
occupational shortages, 38, 96, 97
occupational training, 45, 97
optimal utilization, 97
Organization for Economic Cooperation and Development, 58
outsourcing, 93
overtime, 92

Padoa-Schioppa, Fiorella, 8, 14, 34
Pande, A., 15
Pappone, Jeff, 26, 35
path dependence, 4, 8
perfect information, 5
plant and machine operators and assemblers, 77, 88
politics, institutions and regulations, 59, 62, 64, 66, 67, 82, 84, 87, 89
Portugal, 2, 18, 19, 29, 35, 38, 47, 49, 50, 51, 54, 55, 71, 77, 81, 94, 95, 122
private enterprise, 59, 62, 64
production costs, 21
productivity, 7, 20, 21, 26, 61, 62, 63, 92, 94
public investment, 28

Reich, Robert, 21, 22, 23
replacement demand, 37
Republic of Korea, 2, 17, 18, 19, 21, 22, 29, 38, 46, 47, 49, 54, 55, 81, 124
reservation wage, 7
restrictiveness of labour laws, 59
Richter, M.J., 31, 35
Roberts, Alison, 29, 35, 94, 95
Rodrik, Dani, 16, 23
Roy, R., 26, 34

Sachs, Jeffrey, 16, 23
search costs, 5
secondary education teaching professionals, 84, 85
senior officials, 65, 81
service workers, 71, 88
Sherefkin, Robert, 31, 35
shop and market sales workers, 71, 88
Siebert, Calvin D., 1, 2, 3, 10, 13, 15, 37, 58
Singapore, 2, 16, 18, 19, 30, 34, 35, 38, 46, 47, 49, 52, 54, 55, 69, 74, 125
skill shortages, 1, 4, 16, 22, 25, 26, 28, 29, 31, 33, 36, 88, 93, 94, 97
skilled agricultural and fishery workers, 74
skills transformation, 25
small-scale industries, 29
Snower, D., 4, 7, 13, 14
Solow, Robert M., 4, 7, 10, 14, 15
Spain, 2, 18, 19, 38, 48, 50, 51, 54, 55, 126
Stalker, Peter, 23
static shortages, 4
steady state, 8, 9
Stigler, G., 6, 14
stock options, 26, 93
Sweden, 2, 18, 19, 36, 38, 46, 48, 50, 51, 54, 55, 128

tariff, 20
tax regime, 59, 62, 64
Taylor, K., 21, 23
technical training, 27
technological change, 20
trade, 17, 18, 20, 21, 23, 31, 41, 45, 59, 88
Trutko, John W., 6, 15

Uimonen, T., 34
unemployment rate, 1, 9, 10, 11, 12, 13, 28, 29, 33, 36, 37, 42, 43, 44, 49, 52, 57, 97
unfilled vacancies, 6, 9, 37
United Kingdom, 2, 18, 19, 31, 37, 38, 46, 48, 50, 51, 52, 53, 54, 55, 82, 130
United Nations Conference of Trade and Development, 18, 19
United States, 1, 2, 13, 15, 16, 17, 18, 21, 23, 26, 27, 30, 37, 38, 42, 48, 49,

50, 51, 52, 53, 54, 55, 57, 58, 74, 82, 93, 94, 95, 133
United States Census, 39
unskilled workers, 10
US Department of Labor, Bureau of Labor Statistics, 39, 43, 49, 57, 58

vacancy rate, 9, 10, 37
Veneri, Carolyn M., 30, 35

wage, 2, 4, 6, 7, 8, 31, 36, 42, 44, 53, 56, 69, 85, 91, 92, 93, 97
wage change, 13, 54, 55, 97
wage regulation, 59
Warren, P., 4, 5, 14
Watson, Sharon, 24, 28, 35
Woodall, Pam, 20, 24
Wooldridge, Adrian, 20, 24
writers and creative or performing artists, 85

Yellen, J., 7, 14

Zachary, G. Pascal, 16, 23, 24
Zaidi, Mahmood A., 1, 3, 8, 9, 10, 13, 14, 15, 37, 58